HOW UNIVERSITIES CAN HELP CREATE A WISER WORLD

The Urgent Need for an Academic Revolution

NICHOLAS MAXWELL

SOCIETAS
essays in political
& cultural criticism

imprint-academic.com

Published in the UK by
Imprint Academic, PO Box 200, Exeter EX5 5YX, UK

Distributed in the USA by
Ingram Book Company,
One Ingram Blvd., La Vergne, TN 37086, USA

ISBN 9781845405731

A CIP catalogue record for this book is available from the
British Library and US Library of Congress

Reason, of course, is weak, when measured against its never-ending task.

Albert Einstein

To Christine van Meeteren

Other titles by Nicholas Maxwell:

What's Wrong With Science?
From Knowledge to Wisdom
The Comprehensibility of the Universe
The Human World in the Physical Universe
Is Science Neurotic?
Cutting God in Half – and Putting the Pieces Together Again
With R. Barnett, ed., *Wisdom in the University*
L. McHenry, ed., *Science and the Pursuit of Wisdom: Studies in the Philosophy of Nicholas Maxwell*

Contents

Chapter One

The Basic Idea

Global Crises

The future of humanity is threatened by grave global problems. There is the problem of war, over one hundred million people having been killed in countless wars during the course of the twentieth century (which compares unfavourably with the twelve million or so killed in wars during the nineteenth century).[1] And we have not done very well so far in the 21st century. There is the obscenity of the arms trade, the massive stockpiling of armaments, even by poor countries, and the ever present threat of their use by terrorists or in war, whether the arms be conventional, chemical, biological, or nuclear. There is the sustained, profound injustice of immense differences in wealth around the globe, the industrially advanced first world of North America, Europe, and elsewhere experiencing unprecedented wealth while something like a third of humanity live in conditions of abject poverty in the third world, hungry, unemployed, without proper housing, health care, education, or even access to safe water. There is the long-standing problem of the rapid growth of the world's population, pronounced especially in the poorest parts of the world, and adversely affecting efforts at development. And there is the horror of the AIDS epidemic, again far more terrible in the poorest parts of the world, devastating millions of lives, destroying families, and crippling economies. There is the problem of the progressive destruction of tropical rain forests and other natural habitats, with its concomitant devastating extinction of species. Humanity urgently needs to discover how to create a sustainable world industry and agriculture that does not wreak havoc on the environment; attempts do this have, so far, proved ineffective. There are problems of pollution of air, sea, and earth, and problems of depletion of finite resources. And over everything hangs the menace of climate change, threatening to intensify all the other problems — apart, perhaps, from population growth. (As the climate warms, millions will die. They are dying already.)

Finally, there is what Ronald Higgins, decades ago, called "the seventh enemy": our ingrained incapacity to do what needs to be done to solve our problems.[2]

But it is worse than that. It is not just that our efforts to tackle global problems seem pathetically inadequate. Far worse, much of our efforts seem devoted to *intensifying* our problems. We know that if we continue to emit carbon dioxide at anything like the rate we do at present, we are heading towards disaster. Does this mean we cut back on emissions? All sorts of measures are introduced, but CO_2 emissions actually increase — or only fail to increase because of the world economic recession. High up on the agenda of every government of every nation is economic growth; but it is economic growth, as conducted at present, which leads to higher CO_2 emissions — even if this need not be if power, industry, and transport were run on different, more sustainable lines.

Governments seek security, build up their armies and defence in order to procure security, provoke suspicious neighbour nations to do likewise, and thus increase insecurity and the danger of war.

Banks seek wealth, and plunge the world into debt, recession, and poverty.

Progress is eagerly sought, and the outcome is industrial, agricultural, and population growth beyond what the planet can support. Natural habitats are destroyed, species annihilated, land and sea polluted.

We seem trapped in a vicious nightmare in which what we strive to achieve, our finest and most passionately sought aspirations and ideals, are transformed, as we draw closer to them, into ugly and dangerous monstrosities, threats to our very existence. What we love the most turns out to do us the most harm.

A key example of this nightmare twist is science. Modern science has been pursued, ever since its birth in the 17th century, with the passionate conviction that science will better the lot of humanity. Unquestionably, science has met with quite astonishing intellectual success in improving our knowledge and understanding of the universe, and ourselves as a part of the universe. And modern science and technology have been of immense benefit to humanity. In countless ways, those of us fortunate to live in the wealthy, industrially advanced parts of the world have had our lives enriched beyond the wildest dreams of people living only a couple of centuries ago. Modern science has made possible the modern world.

At the same time, science has helped to create all our current global problems — or at least has made them possible. Science and technology have led to modern industry, agriculture, transport, armaments, medicine, and hygiene. And these in turn have led to global warming, population growth, destruction of natural habitats and rapid extinction of species, the development of extreme inequalities of wealth and power around the globe, pollution of earth, sea, and air, depletion of natural resources, the lethal character of modern war, the increasing threats posed by the spread of modern armaments, and even the AIDS epidemic — AIDS being spread by modern travel.

But it is not just that modern science has made all our global crises possible. It is worse than that. The unprecedented success of modern scientific and technological research is actually the *cause* of our global problems.

At once it will be objected that it is not *science* that is the cause, but rather the things that we *do*, made possible by science and technology. This is obviously correct. But it is also correct to say that scientific and technological progress *is* the cause. The meaning of "cause" is ambiguous. By "the cause" of event E we may mean something like "the most obvious observable events preceding E that figure in the common sense explanation for the occurrence of E". In this sense, human actions (made possible by science) are the cause of such things as people being killed by modern weapons in war, destruction of tropical rain forests. On the other hand, by the "cause" of E we may mean "that prior change in the environment of E which led to the occurrence of E, and without which E would not have occurred". If we put our times into the context of human history, then it is entirely correct to say that, in this sense, scientific-and-technological progress is the cause of our distinctive current global disasters: what has changed, what is new, is scientific knowledge, not human nature. Give a group of chimpanzees rifles and teach them how to use them and in one sense, of course, the cause of the subsequent demise of the group would be the actions of the chimpanzees. But in another obvious sense, the cause would be the sudden availability and use of rifles—the new, lethal technology. Yet again, from the standpoint of theoretical physics, "the cause" of E might be interpreted to mean something like "the physical state of affairs prior to E, throughout a sufficiently large spatial region surrounding the place where E occurs". In this third sense, the sun continuing to shine is as much a part of the cause of war and pollution as human action or modern science and technology.

Some of our most noble efforts and endeavours have led us close to disaster. We strive to procure wealth and happiness for all via economic progress, security via defence, health and longer life via medicine, and a major part of the outcome is climate change, destruction of natural habitats and rapid extinction of species, pollution, depletion of finite natural resources, lethal modern war and the threat of war, and population growth beyond what the earth can sustain. We pursue scientific and technological research out of the noble quest to enhance knowledge and understanding, and to better the lot of humanity, and as a result facilitate all those enterprises that have created our current global problems. Put in even more stark terms, science is actually the *cause* of these problems—in one perfectly legitimate sense of "cause".

No wonder many conclude not just that we cannot make things better, but all our efforts to do so, however nobly and energetically pursued, are doomed just to make things worse. A typical example of someone who thinks along these lines is the very popular writer John Gray who, in book after book, article after article, has argued that progress is illusory, all our efforts to transform the human condition inevitably ending in nightmare.[3]

What Can We Do?

Is there anything we can do to escape this nightmare of even our noblest efforts to make things better ending up making things worse?

There is. In order to make progress towards a better world we need to learn how to do it. And for that, in turn, we need institutions of learning rationally designed and devoted to helping us learn how to solve our global problems, how to make progress towards a better world. It is just this that we lack at present. Our universities are devoted to the pursuit of knowledge. They are neither designed nor devoted to helping humanity learn how to tackle global problems — problems of living — in more intelligent, humane, and effective ways. That is the key disaster of our times, the crisis behind all the others: our failure to have developed our institutions of learning so that they are rationally organized and devoted to helping us solve our problems of living — above all, our global problems. Having universities devoted almost exclusively to the pursuit of knowledge is, as we have seen, a recipe for disaster. Scientific knowledge and technological know-how have unquestionably brought great benefits to humanity. But they have also made possible — even caused — our current global crises.

But is it really conceivable that changing *academia* would make the slightest difference to what goes on in the real world? One meaning of "academic", after all, is "irrelevant", "beside the point". Academics might debate among themselves about what we should do in response to our problems, but why should we suppose they would come up with better solutions than people on the ground, with experience of the real world? Why should we expect them to agree? And even if they did agree, and did come up with good ideas, why should we expect anyone to listen? Would not politics, industry, trade, finance, war, continue on their way, regardless?

Is it even plausible to suppose that academics could agree about what needs to be done to transform universities so that they come to devote themselves to helping humanity learn how to create a better world? Would not right wing academics want one thing, left wing academics another? Would not natural scientists disagree with social scientists, historians disagree with engineers, and philosophers disagree with everyone—above all, with each other? As things are, universities do serve a reasonably decent purpose. They establish facts and add to knowledge; and they train professionals: lawyers, engineers, architects, doctors, and so on. A radical change in the whole structure and character of universities—an academic revolution—would risk sabotaging the good that universities do now, for nothing more fruitful than sterile debate and hot air. The outcome would, in all likelihood, undermine, not assist, humanity in its efforts to make progress towards a better world.

Before I can answer these two objections properly, I must first spell out in outline what it is that I am proposing, and what the reasons are for the proposal.

Urgent Need for an Academic Revolution

The central claim of this book can be put like this.

Academia, as it exists at present, devoted primarily to the pursuit of knowledge, is the outcome of efforts to create a kind of academic inquiry that is rationally organized and devoted to helping humanity achieve what is of value in life, solve problems of living, make social progress towards as good a world as possible. The idea that the fundamental social or humanitarian goal of rational inquiry should be to better the lot of humanity goes all the way back to Francis Bacon in the 17th century. And Bacon helped inspire many of those who created modern science. His writings were inspirational in the creation of the Royal Society in Britain. Natural science—or natural philosophy, as it was known in the 17th century—was pursued in part in the passionate belief that knowledge acquired would help transform the human condition for the better.

The idea was further developed by the Enlightenment of the 18th century, especially by the *philosophes* of the French Enlightenment. Voltaire, Diderot, Condorcet, and the rest had the fundamental and profound idea that it might be possible to learn from scientific progress how to achieve social progress towards an enlightened world. This, correctly interpreted, is the key idea, incidentally, of the present book. In developing this immensely important idea, the *philosophes* took it for granted that in order to put this idea into practice what one needed to do was to develop the social sciences alongside the natural sciences. Francis Bacon had already argued powerfully that, if we wish to achieve social progress, we must acquire authentic knowledge of the natural world. We must do natural science (or natural philosophy). To the *philosophes* it seemed obvious that, if we seek social progress, then it is, if anything, even more important to acquire authentic knowledge of the social world. We need to acquire knowledge of the laws of social development. We need to acquire knowledge of economics, history, and the psychological make-up of people. Knowledge of natural law governing natural phenomena may be important, but even more important is knowledge of social law governing human action and social development.

So the *philosophes* set about creating the *social sciences* alongside the *natural sciences*. They brought into existence, or developed, economics, sociology, psychology, anthropology, political science, history, the study of law, culture, and custom. What the *philosophes* initiated or developed in the 18th century, others — such as J.S. Mill and Karl Marx — further developed throughout the 19th century, often outside universities until, in the early 20th century, social science was built into academic inquiry in universities all over the world with the creation of departments of social science: economics, sociology, anthropology, psychology, political science.

The outcome is what, by and large, we have today, academic inquiry devoted, in the first instance, to the pursuit of knowledge — or *knowledge-inquiry* as we may call it. There are two basic ideas inherent in knowledge-inquiry.

> (1) The primary task for academic inquiry is to acquire knowledge and technological know-how. First, knowledge must be acquired. Once acquired, it can *then* be applied to help solve social problems.
>
> (2) In order to be of value to humanity, knowledge must be objective, factual, and reliable. This means only those considerations relevant to the assessment of knowledge can enter the intellectual domain of inquiry — evidence, valid argument, experimental results, factual claims, empirically testable theories, and the like. Values, ideals, emotions, desires, human hopes and fears, human aspirations, expressions of joy and suffering, policy and political ideas, ideas about how to live — all these must be excluded from the intellectual domain in order to ensure that objective knowledge of fact is obtained. Almost paradoxically, expressions of human aspirations and suffering must be excluded from the intellectual domain, from scientific and scholarly papers, books, and lectures, so that objective, factual knowledge is obtained, alone of human value. If this strict censorship is not observed, knowledge will degenerate into mere propaganda and ideology, and will cease to be of real benefit to humanity.[4]

Knowledge-inquiry, as summarized in (1) and (2), dominates the academic enterprise today.[5] Not all academic work accords with the edicts of knowledge-inquiry, and by no means all academics agree with these edicts — a point to be discussed below. Knowledge-inquiry is, nevertheless, massively influential. It is the dominant paradigm for academia, the only well-known idea as to what constitutes rational inquiry. It is almost unconsciously taken for granted by most academics. It is important to note that knowledge-inquiry does allow that academia may well discuss the *application* of knowledge to help solve social problems. Medicine, biology, engineering, geography, sociology, economics, psychology, political science, the study of international affairs, even though primarily concerned to acquire knowledge, all have applications to human life. Departments of public policy, peace, environment, risk, development, global governance do explore social problems and how they are to be solved. Discussion of what may be called "problems of living" is not excluded from academia, but it has only a secondary role, in accordance with (1) and (2). The primary task of academic inquiry is to solve problems of *knowledge*, not problems of *living*.

Knowledge-inquiry is, however, an intellectual and humanitarian disaster. It is damagingly irrational in a wholesale, structural way. This is the key disaster of our times. It is the gross, structural irrationality of academia that is, in the long term, responsible for the development of our current global problems, and responsible for our incapacity to solve them.

It all goes back to blunders made by the 18th-century Enlightenment. As I have already said, the *philosophes* had the magnificent idea that it might be possible to learn from scientific progress how to achieve social progress towards an enlightened world. But in developing and putting this idea into practice, they made disastrous mistakes, and it is from these mistakes, built into the intellectual/institutional structure of universities today, all over the world, that we still suffer today.

In order to put the Enlightenment idea properly into practice, the following three steps need to be got right.

First, the progress-achieving methods of science need to be correctly identified. *Second*, these methods need to be correctly generalized so that they become fruitfully applicable to any worthwhile, problematic human endeavour, whatever the aims may be, and not just applicable to the endeavour of improving knowledge. And *third*, the correctly generalized progress-achieving methods then need to be exploited correctly in the great human endeavour of trying to make social progress towards an enlightened, wise, civilized world.

Unfortunately, the *philosophes* of the Enlightenment got all three steps wrong. They failed to appreciate that the basic aims of science are profoundly problematic, it being important for science to try to improve its aims and methods as it proceeds. Having failed to capture the progress-achieving methods of science correctly, they naturally failed to generalize them properly, so that they become fruitfully applicable to all worthwhile problematic endeavours, and not just the one endeavour of acquiring knowledge. It is not just in science that basic aims are problematic: this is true in life too. In life we need to try to improve problematic aims, and associated methods, as we act, as we live.

But most disastrously of all, the *philosophes* got the third step wrong. They failed completely to try to apply aim-improving methods, generalized from science, to the immense and profoundly problematic enterprise of making social progress towards an enlightened, wise world. Instead, they sought to apply a seriously defective conception of scientific method to *social science*, to the task of making progress towards, not a *better world*, but to better *knowledge* of social phenomena. They developed social inquiry, not as social *methodology*, designed to help humanity achieve what is of value in life, but rather as social *science*, designed to help academic experts improve knowledge of social phenomena. And it is this ancient blunder, developed throughout the 19th century and built into universities in the early 20th century with the creation of departments of social science, that is responsible for what we have today, knowledge-inquiry in part responsible for the generation of our global problems.[6]

What do we need to do now, in the second decade of the 21st century, to correct the three blunders of the 18th-century Enlightenment?

First, we need to adopt and put into scientific practice a new conception of science which acknowledges the real, highly problematic aims of science. This involves formulating scientific method at what may be called the *meta-methodological* level. Meta-methods specify how the aims and methods of a specific science — or science as a whole — are to be improved in the light of improving knowledge, and other factors. Science adapts its nature, its aims and methods, to what it finds out about the natural world.

Second, we need to generalize this aim-improving, meta-methodology of science so that it becomes fruitfully applicable to *any* worthwhile human endeavour with problematic aims, and not just applicable to the one endeavour of improving knowledge. For, of course, it is not just in science that aims can be problematic: this is the case in life too.

Third, and most important, we need to try to get this aim-improving meta-methodology into the immense and profoundly problematic enterprise of making social progress towards an enlightened, wise world. The aim of such an enterprise is notoriously problematic. For all sorts of reasons, what constitutes a good world, an enlightened, wise, or civilized world, attainable and genuinely desirable, must be inherently and permanently problematic. Here, above all, it is essential to employ methods — meta-methods — which help us improve our aims and make progress when basic aims are problematic.[7]

It is above all our failure to build these aim-improving methods into our social world, into individual, institutional, and global life, that is responsible for the generation of our current global problems. Global warming, rapid population growth, destruction of natural habitats and extinction of species, depletion of natural resources, pollution of earth, air, and sea, the lethal character of modern war, the spread of modern weaponry, intensification of the gulf between the world's wealthy and poor — all these have arisen because of our failure to improve problematic aims of industry, agriculture, politics, finance, the military, trade, international relations. Even the world credit crunch of 2007 and subsequent world economic difficulties fit this pattern. It is not just that we have failed to build into institutions, social fabric, and our way of life aim-improving methods, where aims are inherently problematic. We have not even seen the need to do this. Worse still, we have not even had the *idea* that this is what we need to do. Academia, instead of struggling hard to get the idea understood and implemented, has been preoccupied with quite a different task: the pursuit of knowledge.

As we shall see in the next chapter, the outcome of correcting the three blunders of the *philosophes* is a kind of academic enterprise very different from knowledge-inquiry—what, by and large, we have at present. It would be a kind of academic enterprise more *rigorous* than knowledge-inquiry, of greater *intellectual integrity and value*, and far more *effective* in helping humanity solve problems of living and make progress towards a better world. I shall call this new kind of inquiry *wisdom-inquiry*. It is what emerges when the basic Enlightenment idea is developed and put into practice correctly, without the disastrous three blunders made by the *philosophes*.

I repeat: *the* crisis of our times, the crisis behind all the others, is our failure to have developed a kind of inquiry rationally designed and devoted to helping us solve our problems of living, make progress towards a good, wise, enlightened world —or, at least, towards as good a world as possible. Instead of creating *wisdom-inquiry*, all we have managed to do is create *knowledge-inquiry*, a botched version of wisdom-inquiry.

It is important to appreciate, however, that academia as it exists today, the outcome, by and large, of putting knowledge-inquiry into practice, is a defective version of what we really need: wisdom-inquiry. The task before us is not to create something entirely new, untested, with nothing more to guide us than an abstract philosophical argument. We do not need to leap into the dark blindfolded, as it were, hoping for the best. Rather, our task is to correct quite definite blunders in the structure of academia that we have inherited from the past—blunders we have failed so far to get properly into focus and so put right. We already possess a kind of inquiry created to help us make progress towards a wise, enlightened world: our problem is that we fail to see that the design is defective, and urgently needs to be put right.

Is All This Old Hat?

It may be objected that there is nothing new whatsoever in these criticisms of the Enlightenment, of Science and Rationality. Such criticisms have been voiced for centuries. They go back at least to the Romantic movement of the 18th century.

Long ago, William Blake declared that "Art is the Tree of Life. Science is the Tree of Death" and complained of "single vision and Newton's sleep". Keats lamented that science will "clip an Angel's wings" and "unweave a rainbow". The 18th-century Romantic movement quite generally found science and reason oppressive and destructive, and instead valued art, imagination, inspiration, individual genius, emotional and motivational honesty rather than careful attention to objective fact. Much subsequent opposition to science stems from, or echoes, the Romantic opposition of Blake, Wordsworth, Keats, and many others. There is the movement Isaiah Berlin has described as the "Counter-Enlightenment" (Berlin, 1979, ch. 1). There is existentialism, with its denunciation of the tyranny of reason, its passionate affirmation of the value and centrality of irrationality in human life, from Dostoevsky, Kierkegaard, and Nietzsche to Heidegger and Sartre (see, for example, Barrett, 1962). There is the attack on Enlightenment ideals concerning science and reason undertaken by the Frankfurt School, by post-modernists and others, from Horkheimer and Adorno to Lyotard, Foucault, Habermas, Derrida, MacIntyre, and Rorty (see Gascardi, 1999). The soul-destroying consequences of valuing science and reason too highly is a persistent theme in literature: it is to be found in the works of writers such as D.H. Lawrence, Doris Lessing, Max Frisch, and Y. Zamyatin.[8] There is persistent opposition to modern science and technology, and to scientific rationality, often associated with the Romantic wing of the green movement, and given expression in such popular books as Marcuse's *One Dimensional Man*, Roszak's *Where the Wasteland Ends*, Berman's *The Reenchantment of the World*, and Appleyard's *Understanding the Present*. There is the feminist critique of science and conceptions of science: see, for example, Fox Keller (1984) and Harding (1986). There is Paul Feyerabend's critique of scientific rationality in his *Against Method* (1978) and *Farewell to Reason* (1987). And there are the implications of the so-called "strong programme" in the sociology of knowledge, and of the work of social constructivist historians of science, which depict scientific knowledge as a belief system alongside many other such conflicting systems, having no more right to claim to constitute knowledge of the truth than these rivals, the scientific view of the world being no more than an elaborate myth, a social construct (see Barnes and Bloor, 1981; Bloor, 1991; Barnes, Bloor and Henry, 1996; Shapin and Schaffer, 1985; Shapin, 1994; Pickering, 1984; Latour, 1987). This latter literature provoked a counter-attack by scientists, historians, and philosophers of science seeking to defend science and traditional conceptions of scientific rationality: see Gross and Levitt (1994), and Gross, Levitt and Lewis (1996).

This debate between critics and defenders of science came abruptly to public attention with the publication of Alan Sokal's hoax article 'Transgressing the Boundaries' in a special issue of the cultural studies journal *Social Text* in 1996 entitled *Science Wars*: see Sokal and Bricmont (1998).

For a period, in the late 1990s and early 2000s, the debate became rather widely known as "the science wars" and in its turn received academic attention: see for example, Koertge (1998) and Segerstrale (2000).

There is, then, nothing new in the Enlightenment, science, and reason being subject to critical attack. What does this book have to add to the long-standing debate?

I must stress that the criticisms made here of the Enlightenment, of science, orthodox conceptions of reason, and knowledge-inquiry differ dramatically from the long tradition of Romantic criticism of science and reason just indicated. It is the very opposite of those views and arguments which object to scientific rationality, its scope and influence. My objection to knowledge-inquiry is that it is *irrational*. It is a very damaging kind of irrationality masquerading as rationality. What we need to do is not oppose science and reason, as Romantic criticism would have us believe, but the very opposite; free science from irrational philosophies of science, strengthen and enhance the influence of scientific rationality so that, appropriately generalized, it comes to influence all that we do, all aspects of life, personal, public, institutional, and global. Instead of opposing science, we need to learn from scientific progress how to achieve social progress towards a wiser world. Correct the blunders of the Enlightenment, and the Romantic opposition would become wholly unnecessary: wisdom-inquiry, as I shall show in the next chapter, becomes a kind of synthesis of traditional Rationalism and traditional Romanticism, and a great improvement over both. We suffer, in short, not from too much reason, but from not enough.

The theme and argument of this book is thus diametrically opposed to the long tradition of Romantic opposition to science and reason, from Blake down to today. But it is also at odds with those who defend traditional conceptions of science and reason against Romantic attack. All too often, those who loudly proclaim the virtues of science and reason defend the indefensible, defend irrational conceptions of science, irrational conceptions of reason. They take some version of knowledge-inquiry for granted and fail to see just how damagingly irrational it is.

Far from being old hat, the argument of this book, against knowledge-inquiry and for wisdom-inquiry, differs dramatically from both sides of the rather well-known "science wars" debate. It is very different from Romantic opposition to science and reason; and it is very different from the views of those who defend orthodox conceptions of science and reason from Romantic attack. We urgently need a new way of thinking, a new vision.

All this will be developed in much greater detail as the argument of the book unfolds.

Preliminary Replies to Objections

This summary of my argument that there is an urgent need to bring about an academic revolution may not convince, and may raise more questions than it answers. The argument will be spelled out in more detail in the next chapter. For the moment, suppose that the argument is valid. How does it meet the objections raised at the end of the section before the last one? I now answer those objections, one by one.

Objection: Is it really conceivable that changing *academia* would make the slightest difference to what goes on in the real world? One meaning of "academic", after all, is "irrelevant", "beside the point". **Reply**: This objection, apparently against the significance of transforming academia, actually implies exactly the opposite. Why is academia held to be irrelevant to what goes on in the world? Because, as a result of being shaped and developed to accord with the edicts of knowledge-inquiry, it is all-but specifically designed *not* to interact with and help change the rest of the world. The basic intellectual task of the social sciences and humanities is to improve knowledge of social and cultural phenomena. It is not to help people make progress towards a better world. Knowledge-inquiry requires that the social sciences and humanities should *study* the social world, but not *interfere* or *interact* with it so as to change it. In so far as there is a basic stipulation as to how academia should be related to the rest of the world, it is that the intellectual domain of inquiry should be shielded from the social world so that the pursuit of knowledge is not corrupted by politics, public opinion, and other social pressures and sources of irrationality.

All this would be transformed if wisdom-inquiry was put into practice. The central task of academic inquiry as a whole would be to engage with the rest of the world, with the public, the government, the media, industry, etc. so as to promote more cooperatively rational tackling of problems of living. From the standpoint of wisdom-inquiry, what really matters is the thinking that goes on in the great world beyond academia, guiding personal, institutional, social, and global life. It is this that wisdom-inquiry seeks to help improve, academic thought being but a means to that end. Public education, intelligently conducted by means of argument and discussion, not high-handed instruction, becomes the central concern of universities. Academic inquiry would seek to siphon up good ideas about how to solve problems of living, and good real-life solutions, wherever they are to be found, and then broadcast them as widely as possible, so that they become available to all. Far from primarily seeking to protect the intellectual domain of academia from the corrupting influence of the irrational social world, wisdom-inquiry seeks rather actively to help the social world to become more cooperatively rational.

That academia is at present regarded as somewhat "irrelevant" or "beside the point" is a symptom of its current damaging irrationality. It is a striking indication of the need for change.

Objection: Academics might debate among themselves about what we should do in response to our problems, but why should we suppose they would come up with better solutions than people on the ground, with experience of the real world? **Reply**: Why indeed? As I have already remarked, it would be a primary task of wisdom-inquiry to siphon up good solutions to problems of living wherever they are to be found, and make them as widely available as possible. Knowledge-inquiry demands that one needs to have a Ph.D. before one can make a contribution to academic thought. Wisdom-inquiry carries no such stipulation. Anyone with a good idea can make a contribution, whatever their qualifications, whether educated or not. It is a primary duty of wisdom-inquiry to separate out good ideas from dross, wherever they are to be found, whether within universities or without.

Objection: Why should we expect academics to agree? **Reply**: One of the great responsibilities of wisdom-inquiry academics would be (a) to arrive at some kind of consensus as to what our most important problems of living are, and what we need to do about them, and at the same time (b) to carry on a sustained, lively, imaginative, and critical, intellectually responsible debate about these matters. It is just this that science manages to achieve. On the one hand, there are the agreed results of science — that which is acknowledged to constitute knowledge, observational, experimental, and theoretical, by all scientists. On the other hand, there is the arena of lively debate, where hypotheses are aired and attacked, and even accepted knowledge is severely criticized, everything being subjected to scrutiny. Much of the intellectual success of science is due to the fact that it manages to maintain these two arenas—one of accepted results, the other of furious debate—even though to do so almost involves maintaining a contradiction. A major task of wisdom-inquiry is to establish something similar in connection with ideas about what our problems of living are, and what we need to do about them. I shall have more to say about this in subsequent chapters.

Even if academics failed to reach much agreement, wisdom-inquiry could still be of great value in keeping alive imaginative and critical discussion about what our problems of living are, and what we need to do about them.

Objection: Even if academics did agree, and did come up with good policy ideas, why should we expect anyone to listen? Would not politics, industry, trade, finance, war, continue on their way, regardless? **Reply**: As I have already remarked, academia as conducted today, along the lines of knowledge-inquiry, is all but organized in such a way as to ensure that it has little impact on the rest of the world. Transforming academia so that wisdom-inquiry is put into practice would radically alter this situation. Academia would have, as a central task, to learn from and engage with the rest of the world; academics would no longer be primarily concerned to talk to each other.

Objection: As things are, universities do serve a reasonably decent purpose. They establish facts and add to knowledge; and they train professionals: lawyers, engineers, architects, doctors, and so on. A radical change in the whole structure and character of universities—an academic revolution—would risk sabotaging the good that universities do now, for nothing more fruitful than sterile debate and hot air. The outcome would, in all likelihood, undermine, not assist, humanity in its efforts to make progress towards a better world. **Reply**: In the next chapter I will argue that the pursuit of knowledge can be conducted in a more rigorous way within the framework of wisdom-inquiry than it can be within the framework of knowledge-inquiry. This is because wisdom-inquiry science makes explicit, and so criticizable and improvable, problematic assumptions concerning metaphysics, values, and politics, inherent in the aims of science, that knowledge-inquiry science fails to acknowledge. As a result, wisdom-inquiry science promises to be of greater intellectual and human value than knowledge-inquiry science. To suppose that wisdom-inquiry would produce nothing more worthwhile than sterile debate and hot air is perhaps to over-indulge just a bit in cynicism.

Notes

1   Steven Pinker has argued that violence is steadily decreasing over the centuries, if one takes into account that more and more people are around to kill and be killed: see Pinker (2011). This may be true. Nevertheless, our record of numbers of people killed in war in the 20th and 21st centuries is nothing to be proud of, and the rate at which people are killed goes down all too slowly.
2   Higgins (1978).
3   See for example, Gray (2004).
4   For a very much more detailed exposition of knowledge-inquiry (or "the philosophy of knowledge" as I have also called it) see Maxwell (1984 or 2007a, ch. 2).
5   In my book *From Knowledge to Wisdom*, first published long ago in 1984, I looked at six aspects of academic inquiry to see to what extent knowledge-inquiry dominated the scene. These six aspects consisted of: literature about universities and higher education; the philosophy and sociology of inquiry; pronouncements of scientists; science abstracts; social inquiry; and philosophy: see my (1984, ch. 6). I found that in all these six aspects of academic life knowledge-inquiry was, overwhelmingly, the dominant paradigm. For the second edition, published in 2007, I looked again at these six aspects, and I found that, although there had been some changes, still knowledge-inquiry dominated: see Maxwell (2007a, ch. 6). Since then, I have discussed some recent changes that have taken place in universities that move things a bit in the direction they so urgently need to go, in my view: see Maxwell (2009a; 2012b).
6   For a more detailed formulation of this argument see the next chapter and Maxwell (1984 or 2007a, ch. 2). See also Maxwell (2004a).
7   See works referred to in the previous note.
8   See, for example, Frisch (1974) or Zamyatin (1972).

Chapter Two

Wisdom-Inquiry

We have before us two kinds of inquiry, *knowledge-inquiry* and *wisdom-inquiry*. Both seek to help promote human welfare — help enhance the quality of human life — by intellectual and educational means. Both seek to do this *rationally*. That is, both seek to employ those methods — including the empirical methods of natural science — which give the best hope of yielding results genuinely of value to humanity.

Knowledge-inquiry is what we have inherited from the Enlightenment. The basic *intellectual* aim of knowledge-inquiry is knowledge. First, knowledge is to be acquired; once acquired, it can be applied to help solve social problems.

Knowledge-inquiry demands that a sharp split be made between the social or humanitarian aims of inquiry and the *intellectual* aim. The intellectual aim is to acquire knowledge of truth, nothing being presupposed about the truth. Only those considerations may enter into the intellectual domain of inquiry relevant to the determination of truth — claims to knowledge, results of observation and experiment, arguments designed to establish truth or falsity. Feelings and desires, values, ideals, political and religious views, expressions of hopes and fears, cries of pain, articulation of problems of living: all these must be ruthlessly excluded from the intellectual domain of inquiry as having no relevance to the pursuit of knowledge — although of course inquiry can seek to develop factual knowledge about these things, within psychology, sociology, or anthropology. Within natural science, an even more severe censorship system operates: an idea, in order to enter into the intellectual domain of science, must be an empirically testable claim to factual knowledge.

Knowledge-inquiry excludes values and aspirations from the intellectual domain of inquiry so that authentic, objective, factual knowledge may be acquired instead of mere propaganda and ideology. Almost paradoxically, values and aspirations are excluded so that inquiry can be of genuine human value, and can be capable of helping us realize our human aspirations.[1]

Quite a lot of what goes on in universities today violates basic principles of knowledge-inquiry. On the one hand, there is work in the humanities and some parts of the social sciences, influenced by Romanticism, existentialism, and postmodernism, which is self-consciously anti-rationalist in character. On the other hand, there are some relatively new centres, institutions, and departments in many universities concerned with such things as social policy, environmental problems, development, peace, and well-being which may well be held to constitute the first steps towards wisdom-inquiry, as we shall see in chapter four. Despite this, it is knowledge-inquiry that still dominates academic inquiry today. It is what we have inherited from the past. It is the only well-known idea as to what constitutes rational inquiry. It exercises a massive influence over research, funding, careers, education, university governance, and policy. It has a broader impact on our social world.

Knowledge-inquiry nevertheless has, built into it, the three blunders of the Enlightenment. It is, as a result, damagingly irrational in a structural, wholesale way. Our failure, over the last century or so, to develop a more rational and helpful kind of inquiry is the single most important factor in the genesis of all our current global problems, and our present incapacity to tackle them intelligently, humanely, and effectively.

As I remarked in the last chapter, the Enlightenment, and what it led to, has long been criticized, by the Romantic movement, by what Isaiah Berlin has called "the Counter-Enlightenment", and more recently by the Frankfurt School, by postmodernists, social constructivists, and others. But these standard objections to the Enlightenment and what we have inherited from it are almost the opposite of the criticism I develop here. It is the opposite of all those anti-rationalist, Romantic, and post-modernist views which object to the way the Enlightenment gives far too great an importance to natural science and to scientific rationality. What is wrong with the traditional Enlightenment, and the kind of academic inquiry we now possess derived from it — *knowledge-inquiry* — is not too much "scientific rationality" but, on the contrary, not enough. It is the glaring, wholesale *irrationality* of contemporary academic inquiry, when judged from the standpoint of helping humanity learn how to become more civilized, that is the problem.

Wisdom-inquiry is what results when knowledge-inquiry is modified just sufficiently to cure it of its damaging irrationality by correcting the three blunders we have inherited from the Enlightenment. The basic aim of wisdom-inquiry is wisdom, understood to be the capacity and the active desire to realize what is of value in life, for oneself and others, thus including knowledge, technological know-how, and understanding, but much else besides.[2]

In moving from knowledge-inquiry to wisdom-inquiry much that is good in the former remains unchanged. Nevertheless, almost every branch and aspect of the academic enterprise is affected, and there are major structural changes in the internal organization of academia, and in the way it is related to the rest of the social world — as we shall see.

There are two arguments to show that knowledge-inquiry needs to become wisdom-inquiry in order to be cured of its damaging irrationality. The first argument appeals to *problem-solving* rationality, the second to *aim-pursuing* rationality. The second argument builds on, and improves, the first and, in doing so, further clarifies the character of wisdom-inquiry. I now take these two arguments in turn.

Problem-Solving Rationality

What do I mean by "reason"? As I use the term here, rationality appeals to the idea that there are general methods, rules, or strategies which, if put into practice, give us our best chance, other things being equal, of solving our problems, realizing our aims. Rationality is an aid to success, but does not guarantee success, and does not determine what needs to be done. The rules of reason are *meta*-methodological in character, in that they presuppose that there is much we can successfully do already, and they help us marshal methods implicit in what we can do so as to give us our best chances of solving new, hitherto unsolved problems, attain new, hitherto unattained aims.

Four elementary rules of problem-solving rationality are:

(1) Articulate and seek to improve the articulation of the basic problem(s) to be solved.

(2) Propose and critically assess alternative possible solutions.

(3) When necessary, break up the basic problem to be solved into a number of *specialized* problems — preliminary, simpler, analogous, subordinate problems — (to be tackled in accordance with rules (1) and (2)), in an attempt to work gradually toward a solution to the basic problem to be solved.

(4) Interconnect attempts to solve the basic problem and specialized problems, so that basic problem-solving may guide, and be guided by, specialized problem-solving.

No enterprise which persistently violates (1) to (4) can be judged rational. If academic inquiry is to contribute to the aim of promoting human welfare, the quality of human life, by intellectual means, in a rational way, in a way that gives the best chances of success, then (1) to (4) must be built into the whole institutional/intellectual structure of academic inquiry.

Academic inquiry as it is at present constituted, pursued in accordance with the edicts of knowledge-inquiry, is so grossly irrational that it violates *three* of the above four rules of reason.

In order to see this, two preliminary points need to be noted about the nature of the *problems* that academic inquiry ought to be trying to help solve.

First, granted that academic inquiry has, as its fundamental aim, to help promote human welfare by intellectual and educational means,[3] then the *problems* that inquiry fundamentally ought to try to help solve are problems of living, problems of action. From the standpoint of achieving what is of value in life, it is what we *do*, or refrain from doing, that ultimately matters. Even where new knowledge and technological know-how are relevant to the achievement of what is of value — as they are in medicine or agriculture, for example — it is always what this new knowledge or technological know-how enables us to *do* that matters. All the global problems discussed in the last chapter require, for their resolution, not merely new knowledge, but rather new policies, new institutions, new ways of living. Scientific knowledge and associated technological know-how have, if anything, as we have seen, contributed to the creation of these problems in the first place. Thus problems of living — problems of poverty, ill-health, injustice, deprivation — are solved by what we do, or refrain from doing; they are not solved by the mere provision of some item of knowledge (except when a problem of living *is* a problem of knowledge).

Second, in order to achieve what is of value in life more successfully than we do at present, we need to discover how to resolve conflicts and problems of living in more *cooperatively rational* ways than we do at present. There is a spectrum of ways in which conflicts can be resolved, from murder or all-out war at the violent end of the spectrum, via enslavement, threat of murder or war, threats of a less extreme kind, manipulation, bargaining, voting, to cooperative rationality at the other end of the spectrum, those involved seeking, by rational means, to arrive at that course of action which does the best justice to the interests of all those involved. A basic task for a kind of academic inquiry that seeks to help promote human welfare must be to discover how conflict resolution can be moved away from the violent end of the spectrum towards the cooperatively rational end.

Granted all this, and granted that the above four rules of reason are put into practice then, at the most fundamental level, academic inquiry needs to:

(1) Articulate, and seek to improve the articulation of, personal, social, and global problems of living that need to be solved if the quality of human life is to be enhanced (including those indicated in chapter one);

(2) Propose and critically assess alternative possible solutions — alternative possible *actions, policies, political programmes, legislative proposals, ideologies, philosophies of life.*

In addition, of course, academic inquiry must:

(3) Break up the basic problems of living into subordinate, specialized problems — in particular, specialized problems of knowledge and technology.

(4) Interconnect basic and specialized problem-solving.

Academic inquiry as it mostly exists at present can be regarded as putting (3) into practice to splendid effect. The intricate maze of specialized disciplines devoted to improving knowledge and technological know-how that go to make up current academic inquiry is the result. But, disastrously, what we have at present, academic inquiry implementing knowledge-inquiry, fails to put (1), (2), and (4) into practice. In pursuing knowledge, academic inquiry may articulate problems of knowledge, and propose and critically assess possible solutions, possible claims to knowledge — factual theses, observational and experimental results, theories. But, as we have seen, problems of *knowledge* are not (in general) problems of *living*; and solutions to problems of *knowledge* are not (in general) solutions to problems of *living*. In so far as academia does at present put (1) and (2) into practice, in departments of social science and policy studies, it does so only at the periphery, and not as its central, fundamental intellectual task.

In short, academic inquiry devoted primarily to the pursuit of knowledge, when construed as having the basic humanitarian aim of helping to enhance the quality of human life by intellectual means, fails to put the two most elementary rules of reason into practice (rules (1) and (2)). Academic inquiry fails to do (at a fundamental level) what it most needs to do, namely

(1) articulate problems of living, and (2) propose and critically assess possible solutions. And furthermore, as a result of failing to explore the basic problems that need to be solved, academic inquiry cannot put the fourth rule of rational problem-solving into practice either, namely (4) interconnect basic and specialized problem-solving. As I have remarked, *three* of the four most elementary rules of rational problem-solving are violated.[4]

This gross structural irrationality of contemporary academic inquiry, of knowledge-inquiry, is no mere formal matter. It has profoundly damaging consequences for humanity. As I have pointed out above, granted that our aim is to contribute to human welfare by intellectual means, the basic problems we need to discover how to solve are problems of living, problems of action, not problems of knowledge. In failing to give intellectual priority to problems of living, knowledge-inquiry fails to tackle what most needs to be tackled in order to contribute to human welfare. Knowledge-inquiry cannot do what most needs to be done — propose and critically assess policies, political programmes, philosophies of life — because this does not contribute to *knowledge*. Instead of being at the heart of the academic enterprise, these vital activities are marginalized, pushed to the periphery, or ignored altogether.

Furthermore, in devoting itself to acquiring knowledge in a way that is unrelated to sustained concern about what humanity's most urgent problems are, as a result of failing to put (1) and (2) into practice, and thus failing to put (4) into practice as well, the danger is that scientific and technological research will respond to the interests of scientists themselves and the powerful and the wealthy, rather than to the interests of the poor, of those most in need. Scientists, officially seeking knowledge of truth *per se*, have no official grounds for objecting if those who fund research — governments and industry — decide that the truth to be sought will reflect their interests, rather than the interests of the world's poor. And priorities of scientific research, globally, do indeed reflect the interests of the first world, rather than those of the third world.[5]

Knowledge and technology successfully pursued in a way that is not rationally subordinated to the tackling of more fundamental problems of living, through the failure to put (1), (2), and (4) into practice, is all but bound to lead to the kind of global problems discussed in chapter one, problems that arise as a result of newly acquired powers to act being divorced from the ability to act wisely. The creation of our current global problems, and our inability to respond adequately to these problems, has much to do, in other words, with the long-standing, rarely noticed, structural *irrationality* of our institutions and traditions of learning, devoted as they are to acquiring knowledge dissociated from learning how to tackle our problems of living in more cooperatively rational ways. Knowledge-inquiry, because of its irrationality, is designed to *intensify*, not help *solve*, our current global problems.[6]

Wisdom-Inquiry

Inquiry devoted primarily to the pursuit of knowledge is, then, grossly and damagingly irrational when judged from the standpoint of contributing to human welfare by intellectual means. At once the question arises: What would a kind of inquiry be like that is devoted, in a genuinely rational way, to promoting human welfare by intellectual means? As I have already remarked, I shall call this hypothetical kind of inquiry *wisdom-inquiry*, to stand in contrast to knowledge-inquiry.

As a first step at characterizing wisdom-inquiry, we may take knowledge-inquiry (at its best) and modify it just sufficiently to ensure that all four elementary rules of rational problem-solving, indicated above, are built into its intellectual and institutional structure: see Figure 1.

The primary change that needs to be made is to ensure that academic inquiry implements rules (1) and (2). It becomes the fundamental task of social inquiry and the humanities (1) to articulate, and seek to improve the articulation of, our problems of living, and (2) to propose and critically assess possible solutions, from the standpoint of their practicality and desirability. In particular, social inquiry has the task of discovering how conflicts may be resolved in less violent, more cooperatively rational ways. It also has the task of promoting such tackling of problems of living in the social world beyond academe. Social inquiry is, thus, not primarily social *science*, nor, primarily, concerned to acquire knowledge of the social world; its primary task is to promote more cooperatively rational tackling of problems of living in the social world. Pursued in this way, social inquiry is intellectually more fundamental than the natural and technological sciences, which tackle subordinate problems of knowledge, understanding, and technology, in accordance with rule (3).

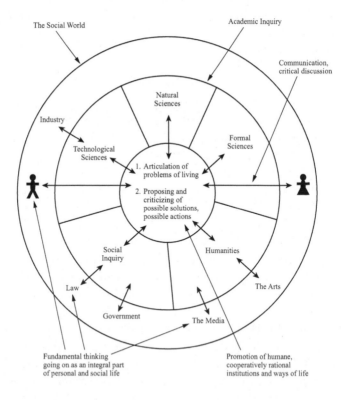

Figure 1: Wisdom-inquiry implementing problem-solving rationality.

In Figure 1, implementation of rule (3) is represented by the specialized problem-solving of the natural, technological, and formal sciences, and more specialized aspects of social inquiry and the humanities. Rule (4) is represented by the two-way arrows linking fundamental and specialized problem-solving, each influencing the other.

One can go further. According to this view, the thinking that we engage in as we live, in seeking to realize what is of value to us, is intellectually more fundamental than the whole of academic inquiry (which has, as its basic purpose, to help cooperatively rational thinking and problem-solving in life to flourish). Academic thought emerges as a kind of specialization of personal and social thinking in life, the result of implementing rule (3); this means there needs to be a two-way interplay of ideas, arguments, and experiences between the social world and academia, in accordance with rule (4). This is represented, in Figure 1, by the two-way arrows linking academic inquiry and the social world.[7]

The natural and technological sciences need to recognize three domains of discussion: evidence, theory, and aims. Discussion of aims seeks to identify that highly problematic region of overlap between that which is discoverable, and that which it is of value to discover. Discussion of what it is of value to discover interacts with social inquiry, in accordance with rule (4).

Wisdom-inquiry as depicted would be more rigorous and of greater human value than knowledge-inquiry because, whereas the latter puts rule (3) into practice but violates rules (1), (2), and (4), the former puts all four rules of reason into practice.

It may be asked: But if academic inquiry today really does suffer from the wholesale structural irrationality just indicated, when and how did this come about? I turn now to a consideration of that question. The answer leads to an improved version of wisdom-inquiry, and to a new argument in support of my claim that wisdom-inquiry, potentially, is more rigorous and of greater human value than knowledge-inquiry.

The Traditional Enlightenment

As we saw briefly in the last chapter, the irrationality of contemporary academic inquiry has its roots in blunders made long ago by the *philosophes* of the 18th-century Enlightenment. I now spell out in more detail what I sketched in chapter one.

A basic idea of the Enlightenment, perhaps *the* basic idea, was to try to learn from scientific progress how to go about making social progress towards an enlightened world. The *philosophes*, Diderot, Helvétius, and others, did what they could to put this immensely important idea into practice, in their lives. They fought dictatorial power, superstition, and injustice with weapons no more lethal than those of argument and wit. They gave their support to the virtues of tolerance, openness to doubt, readiness to learn from criticism and from experience. Courageously and energetically they laboured to promote rationality in personal and social life.[8]

Unfortunately, in developing the Enlightenment idea intellectually, the *philosophes* blundered. They thought the task was to develop the social sciences alongside the natural sciences. I shall call this the *traditional Enlightenment programme*. It was developed throughout the 19th century, by Comte, Marx, Mill, and others, and was built into the institutional structure of universities during the 20th century, with the creation of departments of social science.[9] Knowledge-inquiry, as we have it today, by and large is the result, both natural science and social inquiry being devoted, in the first instance, to the pursuit of knowledge.

But, from the standpoint of creating a kind of inquiry designed to help humanity learn how to become civilized, all this amounts to a series of monumental blunders. These blunders are at the root of the damaging irrationality of current academic inquiry.

The New Enlightenment

In order to implement properly the basic Enlightenment idea of learning from scientific progress how to achieve social progress towards a civilized world, it is essential to get the following three steps right.

1. The progress-achieving methods of science need to be correctly identified.
2. These methods need to be correctly generalized so that they become fruitfully applicable to any worthwhile, problematic human endeavour, whatever the aims may be, and not just applicable to the endeavour of improving knowledge.
3. The correctly generalized progress-achieving methods then need to be exploited correctly in the great human endeavour of trying to make social progress towards an enlightened, wise, civilized world.

Unfortunately, the *philosophes* of the Enlightenment got all three points wrong. And as a result these blunders, undetected and uncorrected, are built into the intellectual-institutional structure of academia as it exists today.[10]

First, the *philosophes* failed to capture correctly the progress-achieving methods of natural science. From d'Alembert in the 18th century to Popper[11] in the 20th, the widely held view, amongst both scientists and philosophers, has been (and continues to be) that science proceeds by assessing theories impartially in the light of evidence, *no permanent assumption being accepted by science about the universe independently of evidence.* Considerations such as simplicity, unity, or explanatory power may legitimately influence choice of theory for a time, but not in such a way that the universe itself, or the phenomena, are assumed to be simple, unified, or comprehensible. This view of *standard empiricism* (as we may call it) is, however, untenable. If taken literally, it would instantly bring science to a standstill. For, given any accepted theory of physics, T, Newtonian theory say, or quantum theory, endlessly many empirically more successful rivals can be concocted which agree with T about observed phenomena but disagree arbitrarily about some unobserved phenomena, and successfully predict phenomena that lie outside the scope of T by means of an additional, independently confirmed law or hypothesis.[12] Physics would be drowned in an ocean of such empirically more successful rival theories.

In practice, these rivals are excluded because they are disastrously disunified. As most upholders of standard empiricism recognize, *two* considerations govern acceptance of theories in physics: empirical success and unity. But in persistently accepting unified theories, to the extent of rejecting disunified rivals that are just as, or even more, empirically successful, physics makes a big persistent assumption about the universe. The universe is such that all disunified theories are false.[13] It has some kind of unified dynamic structure. It is physically comprehensible in the sense that explanations for phenomena exist to be discovered.

But this untestable (and thus metaphysical) assumption that the universe is comprehensible is profoundly problematic. Science is obliged to assume, but does not know, that the universe is physically comprehensible. Much less does it know that the universe is physically comprehensible in this or that way. A glance at the history of physics reveals that ideas have changed dramatically over time. In the 17th century there was the idea that the universe consists of corpuscles, minute billiard balls, which interact only by contact. This gave way to the idea that the universe consists of point-particles surrounded by rigid, spherically symmetrical fields of force, which in turn gave way to the idea that there is one unified self-interacting field, varying smoothly throughout space and time. Nowadays we have the idea that everything is made up of minute quantum strings embedded in ten or eleven dimensions of space-time. Some kind of assumption along these lines must be made but, given the historical record, and given that any such assumption concerns the ultimate nature of the universe, that of which we are most ignorant, it is only reasonable to conclude that it is almost bound to be false.

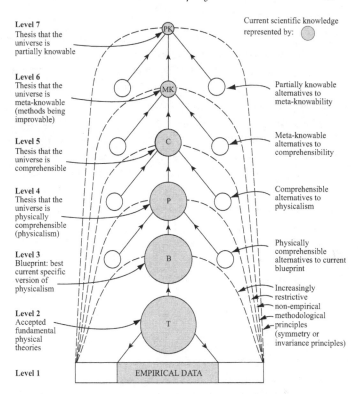

Figure 2: Hierarchical conception of physics of aim-oriented empiricism.

We have here a profound dilemma confronting the scientific enterprise—hidden from view as long as standard empiricism is taken for granted. Science cannot proceed without some kind of assumption concerning the ultimate nature of the universe. This assumption exercises a major influence over science, in influencing both the kind of theories scientists seek to develop, and those they accept. Whether science makes progress or not will depend crucially on how good this assumption is, what sort of justice it does to the nature of the universe. But, just because this assumption is about the ultimate nature of the universe, that of which we are most ignorant, it is almost bound to be false. The historical record backs this point up, in that it reveals we have changed our minds several times about what kind of universe this is, how it is comprehensible. What we must get right, if science is to succeed, we are almost bound to get wrong.

The way to overcome this fundamental dilemma inherent in the scientific enterprise is to adopt a view I have called *aim-oriented empiricism*, which construes physics as making a hierarchy of metaphysical assumptions concerning the comprehensibility and knowability of the universe, these assumptions asserting less and less as one goes up the hierarchy, and thus becoming more and more likely to be true: see Figure 2. In this way a framework of relatively insubstantial, unproblematic, fixed assumptions and associated methods is created within which much more substantial and problematic assumptions and associated methods can be changed, and indeed improved, as scientific knowledge improves. Put another way, a framework of relatively unspecific, unproblematic, fixed *aims* and methods is created within which much more specific and problematic aims and methods evolve as scientific knowledge evolves. (A basic aim of science is to discover in what precise way the universe is comprehensible, this aim evolving as assumptions about comprehensibility evolve.) There is positive feedback between improving knowledge, and improving aims-and-methods, improving knowledge-about-how-to-improve-knowledge. This is the nub of scientific rationality, the methodological key to the unprecedented success of science.[14] Science adapts its nature to what it discovers about the nature of the universe.[15]

Science seeks, not truth *per se* as standard empiricism would have it, but rather truth *presupposed to be explanatory*, or *explanatory* truth. More generally, science seeks *valuable* truth; and this is sought so that it may be *used*, ideally to enrich human life. There are, in other words, profoundly problematic *metaphysical*, *value*, and *political* assumptions inherent in the aims of science; these need sustained critical discussion by scientists and non-scientists alike.[16]

So much for the first blunder of the traditional Enlightenment, and how to put it right.

Second, having failed to identify the methods of science correctly, the *philosophes* naturally failed to generalize these methods properly. They failed to appreciate that the idea of representing the problematic aims (and associated methods) of science in the form of a hierarchy can be generalized and app-lied fruitfully to other worthwhile enterprises besides science. Many other enterprises have problematic aims — problematic because aims conflict, and because what we seek may be unreal-izable, undesirable, or *both*. Such enterprises, with problematic aims, would benefit from employing a hierarchical method-ology, generalized from that of science, thus making it possible to improve aims and methods as the enterprise proceeds. There is the hope that, as a result of exploiting in life methods general-ized from those employed with such success in science, some of the astonishing success of science might be exported into other worthwhile human endeavours, with problematic aims quite different from those of science.

Third, and most disastrously of all, the *philosophes* failed completely to try to apply such generalized, hierarchical prog-ress-achieving methods to the immense, and profoundly prob-lematic, enterprise of making social progress towards an enlightened, wise world. The aim of such an enterprise is notori-ously problematic. For all sorts of reasons, what constitutes a good world, an enlightened, wise, or civilized world, attainable and genuinely desirable, must be inherently and permanently problematic. People have very different ideas as to what does constitute civilization. Most views about what constitutes Utopia, an ideally civilized society, have been unrealizable *and* profoundly undesirable. People's interests, values, and ideals clash. Even values that, one may hold, ought to be a part of civilization may clash. Thus freedom and equality, even though interrelated, may nevertheless clash. It would be an odd notion of individual freedom which held that freedom was for some and not for others; and yet if equality is pursued too single-mindedly this will undermine individual freedom, and will even undermine equality, in that a privileged class will be required to enforce equality on the rest, as in the old Soviet

Union. A basic aim of legislation for civilization, we may well hold, ought to be to increase freedom by restricting it: this brings out the inherently problematic, paradoxical character of the aim of achieving civilization.[17]

Here, above all, it is essential to employ the generalized version of the hierarchical, progress-achieving methods of science, designed specifically to facilitate progress when basic aims are problematic: see Figure 3. It is just this that the *philosophes* failed to do. Instead of applying the hierarchical methodology to *social life*, the *philosophes* sought to apply a seriously defective conception of scientific method to *social science*, to the task of making progress towards, not a *better world*, but better *knowledge* of social phenomena. And this ancient blunder is still built into the institutional and intellectual structure of academia today, inherent in the current character of social science.[18]

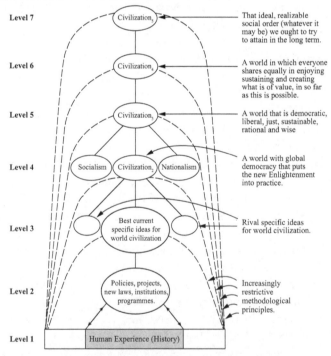

Figure 3: Hierarchical social methodology generalized from science.

Properly implemented, in short, the Enlightenment idea of learning from scientific progress how to achieve social progress towards an enlightened world would involve developing social inquiry, not as social *science*, but as social *methodology*, or social *philosophy*. A basic task would be to get into personal and social life, and into other institutions besides that of science — into government, industry, agriculture, commerce, the media, law, education, international relations — hierarchical, progress-achieving methods (designed to improve problematic aims) arrived at by generalizing the methods of science. A basic task for academic inquiry as a whole would be to help humanity learn how to resolve its conflicts and problems of living in more just, cooperatively rational ways than at present. This task would be intellectually more fundamental than the scientific task of acquiring knowledge. Social inquiry would be intellectually more fundamental than physics. Academia would be a kind of people's civil service, doing openly for the public what actual civil services are supposed to do in secret for governments. Academia would have just sufficient power (but no more) to retain its independence from government, industry, the media, corporations, public opinion, and other centres of power and influence in the social world. It would seek to learn from, educate, and argue with the great social world beyond, but would not dictate. Academic thought would be pursued as a specialized, subordinate part of what is really important and fundamental: the thinking that goes on, individually, socially, and institutionally, in the social world, guiding individual, social, and institutional actions and life. The fundamental intellectual and humanitarian aim of inquiry would be to help humanity acquire wisdom — wisdom being the capacity to realize (apprehend and create) what is of value in life, for oneself and others, wisdom thus including knowledge and technological know-how but much else besides.

One outcome of getting into social and institutional life the kind of aim-evolving, hierarchical methodology indicated above, generalized from science, is that it becomes possible for us to develop and assess rival philosophies of life as a part of social life, somewhat as theories are developed and assessed within science. Such a hierarchical methodology provides a framework within which competing views about what our aims and methods in life should be—competing religious, political, and moral views—may be cooperatively assessed and tested against broadly agreed, unspecific aims (high up in the hierarchy of aims) and the experience of personal and social life. There is the possibility of cooperatively and progressively improving such *philosophies of life* (views about what is of value in life and how it is to be achieved) much as *theories* are cooperatively and progressively improved in science. In science, ideally, theories are critically assessed with respect to each other, with respect to metaphysical ideas concerning the comprehensibility of the universe, and with respect to *experience* (observational and experimental results). In a somewhat analogous way, diverse philosophies of life may be critically assessed with respect to each other, with respect to relatively uncontroversial, agreed ideas about aims and what is of value, and with respect to *experience*—what we do, achieve, fail to achieve, enjoy, and suffer—the aim being to improve philosophies of life (and more specific philosophies of more specific enterprises within life such as government, education, or art) so that they offer greater help with the realization of what is of value in life.[19] This hierarchical methodology is especially relevant to the task of resolving conflicts about aims and ideals, as it helps disentangle agreement (high up in the hierarchy) and disagreement (more likely to be low down in the hierarchy).

Wisdom-inquiry, because of its greater rigour, has intellectual standards that are, in important respects, different from those of knowledge-inquiry. Whereas knowledge-inquiry demands that emotions and desires, values, human ideals and aspirations, philosophies of life be excluded from the intellectual domain of inquiry, wisdom-inquiry requires that they be included. In order to discover what is of value in life it is essential that we attend to our feelings and desires. But not everything we desire is desirable, and not everything that feels good is good. Feelings, desires, and values need to be subjected to critical scrutiny. And of course feelings, desires, and values must not be permitted to influence judgments of factual truth and falsity. Wisdom-inquiry embodies a synthesis of traditional Rationalism and Romanticism. It includes elements from both, and it improves on both. It incorporates Romantic ideals of integrity, having to do with motivational and emotional honesty, honesty about desires and aims; and at the same time it incorporates traditional Rationalist ideals of integrity, having to do with respect for objective fact, knowledge, and valid argument. Traditional Rationalism takes its inspiration from science and method; Romanticism takes its inspiration from art, from imagination, and from passion. Wisdom-inquiry holds art to have a fundamental rational role in inquiry, in revealing what is of value, and unmasking false values; but science, too, is of fundamental importance. What we need, for wisdom, is an interplay of sceptical rationality and emotion, an interplay of mind and heart, "so that we may acquire heartfelt minds and mindful hearts".[20] It is time we healed the great rift in our culture, so graphically depicted by C.P. Snow.[21]

All in all, if the Enlightenment revolution had been carried through properly, the three steps indicated above being correctly implemented, the outcome would have been a kind of academic inquiry very different from what we have at present, inquiry devoted primarily to the intellectual aim of acquiring knowledge.[22] And it is not just academic inquiry that would have been different. With a kind of inquiry rationally devoted to helping us create a wiser world established in universities in democratic countries round the globe, there can be no doubt that our world would now be different—as I shall argue in the next chapter.

Cultural Implications of Wisdom-Inquiry

Wisdom-inquiry does not just do better justice to the social or practical dimension of inquiry than knowledge-inquiry; it does better justice to the "intellectual" or "cultural" aspects as well. The basic aim of wisdom-inquiry is to help us realize what is of value in life, and "realize" means both "apprehend" or "experience" as well as "make real" or "create". In other words, seeking to apprehend, experience, know, or understand for their own sake is just as much a part of the aim as helping us achieve other goals of value to us in life.

One might compare inquiry with sight. Most of us, surely, value seeing for its own sake even more highly than we value seeing for its utilitarian value, its capacity to enable us to find our way around and not bump into things. Discover you are about to lose your sight, and of course distress would come from the practical difficulties that will ensue as a result. But surely by far the greatest distress would come from not being able to experience any more the miraculous visual world — sight for its own sake. A strong argument can be made for holding that we should value the two aspects of inquiry in the same way. However important the practical aspects of inquiry may be, it is the capacity of inquiry to enable us to discover, to explore, to understand, to see valuable aspects of our world for ourselves that is the supremely precious thing. As Einstein is reported to have said, "all our science, measured against reality, is primitive and childlike — and yet it is the most precious thing we have".[23]

From the standpoint of the intellectual or cultural aspect of inquiry, what really matters is the desire that people have to see, to know, to understand the passionate curiosity that individuals have about aspects of the world, and the knowledge and understanding that people acquire and share as a result of actively following up their curiosity. An important task for academic thought in universities is to encourage non-professional thought to flourish outside universities. As Einstein once remarked, "Knowledge exists in two forms — lifeless, stored in books, and alive in the consciousness of men. The second form of existence is after all the essential one; the first, indispensable as it may be, occupies only an inferior position".[24]

Wisdom-inquiry is designed to promote all this in a number of ways. It does so as a result of holding thought, at its most fundamental, to be the personal thinking we engage in as we live. It does so by recognizing that acquiring knowledge and understanding involves articulating and solving personal problems that one encounters in seeking to know and understand. It does so by recognizing that passion, emotion, and desire have a rational role to play in inquiry, disinterested research being a myth. Again, as Einstein has put it, "The most beautiful experience we can have is the mysterious. It is the fundamental emotion which stands at the cradle of true art and true science. Whoever does not know it and can no longer wonder, no longer marvel, is as good as dead, and his eyes are dimmed".[25]

Knowledge-inquiry, by contrast, all too often fails to nourish "the holy curiosity of inquiry",[26] and may even crush it out altogether. Knowledge-inquiry gives no rational role to emotion and desire; passionate curiosity, a sense of mystery, of wonder, have no place, officially, within the rational pursuit of knowledge. The intellectual domain becomes impersonal and split off from personal feelings and desires; it is difficult for "holy curiosity" to flourish in such circumstances. Knowledge-inquiry hardly encourages the view that inquiry at its most fundamental is the thinking that goes on as a part of life; on the contrary, it upholds the idea that fundamental research is highly esoteric, conducted by professional physicists in contexts remote from ordinary life. Even though the aim of inquiry may, officially, be *human* knowledge, the personal and social dimension of this is all too easily lost sight of, and progress in knowledge is conceived of in impersonal terms, stored lifelessly in books and journals. Rare is it for popular books on science to take seriously the task of exploring the fundamental problems of a science in as accessible, non-technical, and intellectually responsible a way as possible.[27] Such work is not highly regarded by knowledge-inquiry, as it is deemed not to contribute to "expert knowledge". The failure of knowledge-inquiry to take seriously the highly problematic nature of the aims of inquiry leads to insensitivity as to what aims are being pursued, to a kind of institutional hypocrisy. Officially, knowledge is being sought "for its own sake", but actually the goal may be immortality, fame, the flourishing of one's career or research group, as the existence of bitter priority disputes in science indicates. Education suffers.

Science students are taught a mass of established scientific knowledge, but may not be informed of the *problems* which gave rise to this knowledge, the problems which scientists grappled with in creating the knowledge. Even more rarely are students encouraged themselves to grapple with such problems. And rare, too, is it for students to be encouraged to articulate their own problems of understanding that must, inevitably, arise in absorbing all this information, or to articulate their instinctive criticisms of the received body of knowledge.[28] All this tends to reduce education to a kind of intellectual indoctrination, and serves to kill "holy curiosity". Officially, courses in universities divide up into those that are vocational, like engineering, medicine, and law, and those that are purely educational, like physics, philosophy, or history. What is not noticed, again through insensitivity to problematic aims, is that the supposedly purely educational are actually vocational as well: the student is being trained to be an academic physicist, philosopher, or historian, even though only a minute percentage of the students will go on to become academics. Real education, which must be open-ended, and without any predetermined goal, rarely exists in universities, and yet few notice.[29]

In order to enhance our understanding of persons as beings of value, potentially and actually, we need to understand them empathetically, by putting ourselves imaginatively into their shoes and experiencing, in imagination, what they feel, think, desire, fear, plan, see, love, and hate. For wisdom-inquiry, this kind of empathic understanding is rational and intellectually fundamental. Articulating problems of living and proposing and assessing possible solutions is, we have seen, the fundamental intellectual activity of wisdom-inquiry. But it is just this that we need to do to acquire empathic understanding. Social inquiry, in tackling problems of living, is also promoting empathic understanding of people. Empathic understanding is essential to wisdom. Elsewhere I have argued, indeed, that empathic understanding plays an essential role in the evolution of consciousness. It is required for cooperative action, and even for science.[30]

Granted knowledge-inquiry, on the other hand, empathic understanding hardly satisfies basic requirements for being an intellectually legitimate kind of explanation and understanding. It has the status merely of "folk psychology", on a par with "folk physics".[31]

Finally, the hierarchical conception of science, illustrated in Figure 2 above, does much better justice to the scientific search for explanation and understanding than does standard empiricism. For, according to standard empiricism, a physical theory, in order to be acceptable, must satisfy empirical requirements only. Failing to be explanatory hardly counts as valid scientific grounds for rejecting a theory, if it is sufficiently empirically successful. The hierarchical view, on the other hand, demands that a physical theory, in addition to being sufficiently empirically successful, must be unified — that is, explanatory — if it is to be acceptable. The search for explanation and understanding is built into the methodology of the hierarchical view of aim-oriented empiricism.[32]

This difference has had implications for physics itself. Orthodox quantum theory is an extraordinarily successful theory empirically. This suffices, granted standard empiricism (the generally accepted view), to render orthodox quantum theory an acceptable theory. And indeed for decades almost all physicists held orthodox quantum theory to be a firmly established part of theoretical knowledge in physics, on empirical grounds. Orthodox quantum theory is, however, a theory not about such entities as electrons and atoms *per se*; rather, it is a theory that makes predictions about the results of performing measurements on these entities. This means orthodox quantum theory is made up of two incoherent parts: a quantum theoretic part, and a part taken from classical physics to describe measurement. This means orthodox quantum theory is very seriously *disunified*. It fails to be *explanatory* in character, because of this lack of unity. Granted aim-oriented empiricism, orthodox quantum theory is unacceptable, despite its great empirical success, because of its lack of unity, its failure to be explanatory. And indeed, a few physicists regarded orthodox quantum theory as, ultimately, unacceptable, somewhat on these grounds—most famously, Einstein and Schrödinger. It may well be that long-standing acceptance of orthodox quantum theory, and the general failure to see the theory as problematic (because non-explanatory)—as a result of general acceptance of standard empiricism—has served to impede progress in physics from the time quantum theory was first discovered, in 1925 and 1926.[33]

Knowledge Before Action?

The entire argument for wisdom-inquiry as it has been developed so far faces a very obvious objection. How can it be rational—even possible—to tackle problems of living before relevant knowledge has been acquired? It must be correct to acquire knowledge first, before we can begin to consider what to do to solve our problems of living. How could we even know what our problems of living are if we did not first have knowledge about the circumstances and conditions that give rise to these problems? The prescriptions of knowledge-inquiry are correct, and wisdom-inquiry is a fantasy, and would be a disaster if ever implemented.

I have six replies to this objection.

First, even if the objection were valid, it would still be vital for a kind of inquiry designed to help us build a better world to include rational exploration of problems of living, and to ensure that this guides priorities of scientific research (and is guided by the results of such research).

Second, the validity of the objection becomes dubious when we take into account the considerable success people met with in solving problems of living in a state of extreme ignorance, before the advent of science. We still today often arrive at solutions to problems of living in ignorance of relevant facts.

Third, the objection is not valid. In order to articulate problems of living and explore imaginatively and critically possible solutions (in accordance with problem-solving rationality) we need to be able to act in the world, imagine possible actions, and share our imaginings with others: in so far as some common sense knowledge is implicit in all this, such knowledge is required to tackle rationally and successfully problems of living. But this does not mean that we must give intellectual priority to acquiring new relevant knowledge before we can be in a position to tackle rationally our problems of living.

Fourth, simply in order to have some idea of what kind of knowledge or know-how it is *relevant* for us to try to acquire, we must *first* have some provisional ideas as to what our problem of living is and what we might do to solve it. Articulating our problem of living and proposing and critically assessing possible solutions needs to be intellectually prior to acquiring relevant knowledge simply for this reason: we cannot know what new knowledge it is *relevant* for us to acquire until we have at least a preliminary idea as to what our problem of living is, and what we propose to do about it. A slight change in the way we construe our problem may lead to a drastic change in the kind of knowledge it is relevant to acquire. Changing the way we construe problems of health to include *prevention* of disease (and not just curing of disease) leads to a dramatic change in the kind of knowledge we need to acquire (importance of exercise, diet, etc.). Including the importance of avoiding *pollution* in the problem of creating wealth by means of industrial development leads to the need to develop entirely new kinds of knowledge.

Fifth, relevant knowledge is often hard to acquire; it would be a disaster if we suspended life until it had been acquired. Knowledge of how our brains work is presumably highly relevant to all that we do but, clearly, suspending rational tackling of problems of living until this relevant knowledge has been acquired would not be a sensible step to take. It would, in any case, make it impossible for us to acquire the relevant knowledge (since this requires scientists to act in doing research). Scientific research is itself a kind of action carried on in a state of relative ignorance.

Sixth, the capacity to act, to live, more or less successfully in the world, is more fundamental than (propositional) knowledge. Put in Rylean terms, "knowing how" is more fundamental than "knowing that".[34] All our knowledge is but a development of our capacity to act. Dissociated from life, from action, knowledge stored in libraries is just paper and ink, devoid of meaning. In this sense, problems of living are more fundamental than problems of knowledge (which are but an aspect of problems of living); giving intellectual priority to problems of living quite properly reflects this point.[35]

In seeking to acquire knowledge of the social world, we have before us the following choice.

On the one hand, we may implement wisdom-inquiry, give intellectual priority to the rational tackling of problems of living and, in an intellectually secondary way, seek to acquire that knowledge of the social world which helps sustain the primary task of tackling problems of living. For example, given that the problem of living we seek to solve is poverty, we set out to acquire knowledge which helps clarify the nature and extent of the problem, and which helps assess critically proposals as to what needs to be done to solve or ameliorate the problem. That knowledge of social phenomena is sought which helps sustain and promote the primary task: the rational tackling of problems of living.

On the other hand, we may attempt to implement knowledge-inquiry, and seek to acquire knowledge of social phenomena in a way that is dissociated from prior concern with problems of living—the idea being that, once knowledge is obtained, it can be applied to help solve social problems.

My claim is that the wisdom-inquiry approach is more rigorous, more objective, and likely to be more successful than the knowledge-inquiry approach, because it makes explicit, and so criticizable and improvable, what the knowledge-inquiry approach leaves implicit, uncriticizable, and so, in all likelihood, unimproved. Knowledge-inquiry social science will cluster the pursuit of knowledge around problems of living, but these latter will be left unarticulated, bereft of imaginative and critical exploration. Priorities of research become mere dogmas rather than critically scrutinized conjectures. What ought to be the primary intellectual activity—imaginative and critical exploration of problems of living and their possible solutions—is relegated to a secondary activity, if engaged in at all. Wisdom-inquiry social science reverses all this. Priority is given to the intellectual exploration of problems of living. The pursuit of knowledge is, quite explicitly, conducted as a secondary activity, as an aid and adjunct to the primary task. Whereas wisdom-social-inquiry puts our problems of living at the heart of the enterprise, knowledge-social-science relegates these problems to the periphery, or suppresses discussion of them altogether, progress towards a wiser world being sabotaged as a result.

Natural and Social Science

Does this argument mean that the pursuit of knowledge ought always to be subordinated to the pursuit of practical problems of living? Does wisdom-inquiry demand that knowledge is never sought in a way that is dissociated from a more fundamental concern with practical problems of living? No. Wisdom-inquiry holds that the pursuit of knowledge, dissociated from any concern to help solve practical problems of living is, to a limited extent, justified.

In the first place, as I argued in the section before the last one, wisdom-inquiry emphatically supports the pursuit of knowledge, explanation, and understanding for their own sake, as being of value in their own right in our lives. A primary task for academic inquiry is to help us to see, to know, to understand significant aspects of the world around us. Wisdom-inquiry does not just support research pursued for its own sake; it does better justice to this vital aspect of inquiry than knowledge-inquiry does—as we saw in the section before the last. And this applies just as much to the social sciences and the humanities as to natural science. Problems of knowledge may, in other words, be personal problems of living in their own right—problems of personal seeing, knowing, understanding.

In the second place, open-ended, curiosity-driven research deserves to be encouraged because it can happen that problems are solved indirectly, and not by means of a direct attack. We need, for this reason alone if for no other, to keep alive traditions of explorative research—the idea being that we may, in this way, stumble across solutions to urgent practical problems that could not be solved by means of direct assault. Curiosity-driven research may even serve to reveal the existence of urgent practical problems of living which we would not otherwise have been aware of. Our awareness of the impending menace of global warming may well have been discovered in this way. We became aware of global warming, it may be argued, because of research conducted into polar ice, glaciers, land, sea, and atmosphere initially without any idea that this would reveal that the planet is getting warmer.

In the third place, special considerations arise in connection with natural science, which justify the search for knowledge and understanding in a way that is unrelated to any concern for practical problems of living *even if our ultimate hope is to make discoveries which will help solve practical problems of living*. These special considerations do not arise, however, in connection with the social sciences. In this crucial respect, the natural and social sciences differ dramatically. Pure research conducted in the hope that there will eventually be unsuspected practical applications is justified as far as natural science is concerned, but not justified as far as social science is concerned.

From the outset, modern science was based on the idea that we are profoundly ignorant of the ultimate nature of the physical universe. But not entirely ignorant. We have a kind of skeleton knowledge of its nature, sufficient to provide a framework for scientific research. The whole enterprise of natural science presupposes that the universe is physically comprehensible in some way or other—as we have seen. There exists a physical *something*—a kind of physical field—present everywhere, in all phenomena, at all times, in an unchanging way which, together with instantaneous, changing states of affairs, determines, perhaps probabilistically, how instantaneous states of affairs evolve. This presupposition tells us that we are ignorant about the nature of the universe, in a quite specific way. We have some *knowledge* about the domain of our ignorance, and it is this skeleton knowledge which specifies, in more or less general terms, what the aims and methods of natural science need to be in order to meet with success.

In other words, quite independent of our human problems of living, natural science has an agenda for research, set for it by its metaphysical presupposition. It makes sense to seek knowledge and understanding of the natural world in a way that is unrelated to any effort or concern to solve specific problems of living. Again and again, research in natural science that has sought no more than knowledge, explanation, and understanding for their own sake has led subsequently to entirely unforeseen and extraordinarily fruitful technological applications—to the solutions to problems of living which no one, beforehand, could even guess might one day be solved. Michael Faraday's discovery of the electric motor and dynamo falls into this category. So does Wilhelm Röntgen's discovery of X-rays. Research that sought to solve the problem of taking photographs of bones inside living bodies would not, in the absence of knowledge of X-rays, have got anywhere, and would not have led to the discovery of X-rays. We might call this capacity of natural science to make discoveries that turn out, after the event, to be extraordinarily fruitful for all sorts of practical applications in an entirely unanticipated way, "the Faraday effect".

No comparable examples of the Faraday effect from social science come to mind, and it is all but impossible even to imagine how such a thing could come about. The specific considerations which make it important to pursue pure research in natural science unconstrained by, and without thought for, practical applications are just not relevant when it comes to social science. As far as our human world is concerned, there is nothing comparable to the presupposition of natural science that the universe is physically comprehensible. In the case of the human world, we are what we study. We already possess knowledge and understanding of ourselves. We are not entirely removed from ourselves, alien to ourselves, in the way that the ultimate nature of the physical universe is alien to us, and unknown to us. And what we are, how we live, the nature of social reality, is not fixed for all time. We change, we learn, we make progress. Nothing in the social world corresponds to the fixed, unchanging nature of the physical universe which, in some unknown way, determines (perhaps probabilistically) everything that occurs, down to the minutest detail. Human nature, societies, and cultures are no doubt not infinitely variable in character. Nevertheless, whatever fixed character they may have, it is quite different from what physics presupposes to exist in the universe. There would seem to be no basis, in other words, to hold that there are specifically social or human laws, which apply to the human world, in the way that there are physical or natural laws that apply to the natural world. As social scientists sometimes comment, given that a basic aim of social science is to help humanity make progress, improve the human condition, there is something very odd indeed about basing social science on the idea that the human world has a fixed, underlying reality — as if we are as removed from ourselves as the moon is, or the electromagnetic field, or the cosmos.

Another factor that brings out this difference between natural and social science is the very different extents to which the two domains produce theories that are genuinely explanatory. Physical theories are powerfully explanatory, partly because of their universality of applicability (they apply at all times and places), partly because they are *unified* — they attribute the same dynamical laws to all the phenomena to which they apply — and partly because they are richly counterfactual in character. Whenever a physical theory is applied to some state of affairs to predict how it will evolve, the theory also predicts how the state of affairs would have evolved if the initial conditions had been different in infinitely many different ways. Newtonian theory, applied to a cannonball shot at such-and-such an angle with such-and-such initial velocity does not just predict the path the cannonball will follow; it also predicts endlessly many different paths the ball would have followed if the initial angle and velocity had been different in such-and-such ways. By contrast, theories in the social sciences lack all three features required of a theory in order to be genuinely explanatory. They lack universality of applicability — not, perhaps, a serious failing in theories intended to apply only to the human world. They lack the degree of unity achieved by physical theory—a rather more serious failing. But most serious of all, theories in the social sciences fail to make predictions about a range of counterfactual state of affairs. Even in economics, generally acknowledged to be that social science which comes closest in character to natural science, counterfactual predictions are hotly contested by rival factions of economists—a state of affairs that is inconceivable in physical science. In other social sciences, reliable counterfactual predictions, on the basis of theory, are even harder to come by. Some historians attempt to do counterfactual history but, very strikingly, many historians question whether such a field has any legitimacy and, in any case, no reliable counterfactual predictions are forthcoming from historical or sociological theory.

In so far as there is a metaphysical presupposition for social science that is somewhat comparable to the metaphysical pre-supposition of underlying unity of natural science, it is, perhaps, the thesis that our human world has come to be as a result of Darwinian evolution, evolution by cultural means, and history. This would involve, in part, construing human beings as pursu-ing the basic goals of survival and reproductive success, these goals being interpreted in a variety of ways, however, as a result of the evolution of imagination, language, consciousness, and human culture. Reproductive success might come to be inter-preted as reproduction of self via perpetuation of social and cultural artefacts: firms, buildings, works of art, scientific theories, institutions, laws, customs, even nations. The suicide terrorist may seem to be violating Darwinian edicts of survival and reproductive success but, for the terrorist himself, his act of suicide may be an heroic act of survival, in that it takes him straight to heaven and eternal survival.

There is an important additional argument against pursuing social science on analogy with natural science by, first, acquiring knowledge, and then applying it to help solve social problems. Not only is this unlikely to meet with much success, because the social world and our relationship to it differ so dramatically from the physical universe and our relationship to it. In addition, this procedure, were it to be successful in the social realm, would be of questionable morality. What is involved in the natural sciences is the manipulation of bits of the natural world to produce technology that, ideally, serves our best interests. Manipulating nature is, in itself, morally neutral — unless there are adverse consequences for life (or unless "the bits of nature" we manipulate include life). But the equivalent procedure in social science would be very different. This would involve manipulating *people* to serve our best interests. Perhaps some manipulation of people is morally justifiable. Governments may be justified in taking steps to stimulate economic activity in times of recession, for example — people being manipulated to produce and purchase. But manipulation should not be the primary way in which we seek to interact with one another. By contrast, wisdom-inquiry gives priority, not to manipulation, but to cooperation. If you and I are to cooperate, we must be able to understand each other, appreciate each other's objectives, plans, desires, intentions, problems, beliefs, values, hopes, and fears — those relevant, at least, to our joint venture. We must be able to acquire empathic understanding of each other. That is, we must be able to articulate each other's problems of action, and each other's ideas as to what might be done in response to them. But it is just this kind of thinking that lies at the heart of wisdom-inquiry. Wisdom-inquiry puts cooperation, and the kind of mutual understanding required for cooperation to flourish, at centre stage. Knowledge-inquiry social science, by contrast, is designed to promote manipulation rather than cooperation, and is, as a result, flawed morally to its core.[36]

In this section I have qualified slightly the overall argument of this book. It is not always the case that the pursuit of knowledge needs to be directly related to, conducted as a subordinate aspect of, efforts to solve problems of living. *Even if our concern is ultimately to help solve problems of living*, it nevertheless makes sense to pursue research in natural science in a way that is detached from any immediate concern with any specific problem of living. This is because the metaphysical presuppositions of natural science set an agenda for research. Acquiring knowledge and understanding of natural phenomena, without any thought for practical applications, may nevertheless subsequently lead to fruitful applications which could never have been anticipated, and which could not have been discovered by means of a direct assault — as the case of the medical use of X-rays illustrates. These special considerations that arise in connection with natural science do not arise, however, in connection with social science. Here, the elementary requirement of rational problem-solving applies in an unqualified way. The pursuit of knowledge and understanding of our human world does need to be related to concern for our problems of living. To suppose otherwise is to reproduce the great blunder of the 18th-century Enlightenment.

I must now add one or two qualifications to the qualification I have just summarized.

First, psychology, or neuroscience, may be an exception to the general point I have made about social science. In the case of psychology there is a definite, still little understood structure that underpins all mental phenomena, and that is associated with all human behaviour, namely the living human brain. This is capable, perhaps, of performing for psychology a function similar to that which the physically comprehensible structure of the universe performs for physics.

Secondly, even though it makes sense to fund pure research in natural science even though there are no obvious practical outcomes, in the hope that entirely unexpected practical outcomes will, nevertheless, eventually emerge, it needs also to be recognized that, quite correctly and properly, an enormous volume of research in the natural sciences does have practical outcomes in mind. Much scientific research seeks to acquire knowledge directly related to human concerns, having to do with health, transport, communications, energy production, and so on. Here, scientific problems of knowledge are a subordinate part of more fundamental human problems of living. We seek to solve the scientific problems of knowledge as an aid to solving the problems of living. Assumptions concerning values and human use, inherent in scientific research aims and priorities, need to be imaginatively and critically explored in a sustained way, as an integral part of social inquiry, and in a way that is open to public participation—as stipulated by aim-oriented empiricism and wisdom-inquiry.

Thirdly, it may be tempting to hold that, in natural science, pure research comes first, then applied research, and then, last, technological research and development. But this view of the matter is untenable. Sometimes new technology comes first, and then, subsequently, prompts developments in pure scientific knowledge. The most famous example is, perhaps, that of the steam engine which, in the hands of Sadi Carnot, led to the founding of thermodynamics. Problems of living, new technological discoveries and developments, and pure research in science are inextricably interlinked, influences going in both directions.

Fourthly, there are reasons for holding that the Faraday effect[37] may become far less prominent as our scientific knowledge and understanding improve. Compare Faraday's research into what was perhaps *the* fundamental problem of theoretical physics of his time, the relationship between electricity and magnetism, with research into the fundamental problem of our time, unification of quantum theory and general relativity. Faraday spectacularly improved our knowledge and understanding of low-energy phenomena associated with our immediate environment. His discoveries led to the development of the electric motor and dynamo. The discovery of the theory that unifies quantum theory and general relativity is, however, very unlikely to have such fruitful practical implications. It is more than likely that the theory that unifies quantum theory and general relativity will only yield startlingly new predictions in conditions of extremely high energy-density, ordinarily only encountered close to the big bang (and perhaps inside black holes). It is not easy to see how such a theory could lead to the development of useful new technology.

I conclude this section with a word about the history of discussion of the nature and methods of the natural and social sciences. It is customary to divide views up into *pro-naturalists* and *anti-naturalists*.[38] The pro-naturalists hold that social science has methods and a character that is similar to that of natural science, whereas the anti-naturalists hold the opposite: the two kinds of science are different. Anti-naturalists may argue, for example, that in doing social science we study *ourselves*; we seek empathic *understanding* of a kind quite different from anything sought in natural science.

Wisdom-inquiry breaks the mould. It holds that there is one overall methodology for all of inquiry: problem-solving rationality and aim-oriented rationality. But it also holds that social inquiry is fundamentally different from natural science. Social inquiry seeks to develop and assess not *theories*, not *factual claims to knowledge*, but rather *policies, proposals for action*, intended, if implemented, to help solve problems of living, help people realize what is of value in life. As far as wisdom-inquiry is concerned, social inquiry is not, fundamentally, science at all. It is not even, primarily, devoted to improving *knowledge* or *understanding*. It has as its basic task, as I have said, to help us resolve our problems of living in more just, peaceful, cooperatively rational, wise ways. Problems of knowledge and understanding are tackled in a subordinate fashion, to bring to light the existence of problems of living and clarify their nature, and to assist in the task of developing and critically assessing policy, proposals as to how these problems may be resolved. What *explanatory theory* is within natural science, so *proposal for action* is within social inquiry. Other differences between natural science and social inquiry all arise as a result of this fundamental difference: in the one case we seek to solve problems of knowledge, in the other we seek to help solve problems of living.

What Needs to be Done to Transform Knowledge-Inquiry into Wisdom-Inquiry

Here is a list of changes that need to be made to knowledge-inquiry if it is to become wisdom-inquiry.

1. There needs to be a change in the basic intellectual *aim* of inquiry, from the growth of knowledge to the growth of wisdom — wisdom being taken to be the capacity to realize what is of value in life, for oneself and others, and thus including knowledge, understanding, and technological know-how (but much else besides).

2. There needs to be a change in the nature of academic *problems*, so that problems of living are included, as well as problems of knowledge — the former being treated as intellectually more fundamental than the latter.

3. There needs to be a change in the nature of academic *ideas*, so that proposals for action are included as well as claims to knowledge — the former, again, being treated as intellectually more fundamental than the latter.

4. There needs to be a change in what constitutes intellectual *progress*, so that progress-in-ideas-relevant-to-achieving-a-more-civilized-world is included as well as progress in knowledge, the former being indeed intellectually fundamental.

5. There needs to be a change in the idea as to where inquiry, at its most fundamental, is located. It is not esoteric theoretical physics, but rather the thinking we engage in as we seek to achieve what is of value in life. Academic thought is a (vital) adjunct to what really matters, personal and social thought active in life.

6. There needs to be a dramatic change in the nature of social inquiry (reflecting points 1 to 5). Economics, politics, sociology, and so on, are not, fundamentally, *sciences*, and do not, fundamentally, have the task of improving knowledge about social phenomena. Instead, their task is threefold. First, it is to articulate problems of living, and propose and critically assess possible solutions, possible actions or policies, from the standpoint of their capacity, if implemented, to promote wiser ways of living. Second, it is to promote such cooperatively rational tackling of problems of living throughout the social world. And third, at a more basic and long term level, it is to help build the hierarchical structure

of aims and methods of aim-oriented rationality into personal, institutional, and global life, thus creating frameworks within which progressive improvement of personal and social life aims-and-methods becomes possible. These three tasks are undertaken in order to promote cooperative tackling of problems of living—but also in order to enhance empathic or "personalistic" understanding between people as something of value in its own right. Acquiring knowledge of social phenomena is a vital but subordinate activity, engaged in to facilitate the above three fundamental pursuits.

7. Natural science needs to change, so that it includes at least three levels of discussion: evidence, theory, and research aims. Discussion of aims needs to bring together scientific, metaphysical, and evaluative consideration in an attempt to discover the most desirable and realizable research aims. It needs to influence, and be influenced by, exploration of problems of living undertaken by social inquiry and the humanities, and the public.

8. There needs to be a dramatic change in the relationship between social inquiry and natural science, so that social inquiry becomes intellectually more fundamental from the standpoint of tackling problems of living, promoting wisdom. Social inquiry influences choice of research aims for the natural and technological sciences, and is, of course, in turn influenced by the results of such research. (Social inquiry also, of course, conducts empirical research, in order to improve our understanding of what our problems of living are, and in order to assess policy ideas whenever possible.)

9. The current emphasis on specialized research needs to change so that sustained discussion and tackling of broad, global problems that cut across academic specialities is included, both influencing and being influenced by specialized research.

10. Academia needs to include sustained imaginative and critical exploration of possible futures, for each country, and

for humanity as a whole, policy and research implications being discussed as well.

11. The way in which academic inquiry as a whole is related to the rest of the human world needs to change dramatically. Instead of being intellectually dissociated from the rest of society, academic inquiry needs to be communicating with, learning from, teaching, and arguing with the rest of society — in such a way as to promote cooperative rationality and social wisdom. Academia needs to have just sufficient power to retain its independence from the pressures of government, industry, the military, and public opinion, but no more. Academia becomes a kind of civil service for the public, doing openly and independently what actual civil services are supposed to do in secret for governments.

12. There needs to be a change in the role that political and religious ideas, works of art, expressions of feelings, desires, and values have within rational inquiry. Instead of being excluded, they need to be explicitly included and critically assessed, as possible indications and revelations of what is of value, and as unmasking of fraudulent values in satire and parody, vital ingredients of wisdom.

13. There need to be changes in education so that, for example, seminars devoted to the cooperative, imaginative, and critical discussion of problems of living are at the heart of all education from five-year-olds onwards. Politics, which cannot be taught by knowledge-inquiry, becomes central to wisdom-inquiry, political creeds and actions being subjected to imaginative and critical scrutiny.

14. There need to be changes in the aims, priorities, and character of pure science and scholarship, so that it is the curiosity, the seeing and searching, the knowing and under-standing of individual persons that ultimately matters, the more impersonal, esoteric, purely intellectual aspects of science and scholarship being means to this end. Social inquiry needs to give intellectual priority to helping empathic understanding between people to flourish (as indicated in 6 above).

15. There need to be changes in the way mathematics is understood, pursued, and taught. Mathematics is not a branch of knowledge at all. Rather, it is concerned to explore problematic *possibilities*, and to develop, systematize, and unify problem-solving methods.[39]

16. Literature needs to be put close to the heart of rational inquiry, in that it explores imaginatively our most profound problems of living and aids personalistic understanding in life by enhancing our ability to enter imaginatively into the problems and lives of others.

17. Philosophy needs to change so that it ceases to be just another specialized discipline and becomes instead that aspect of inquiry as a whole that is concerned with our most general and fundamental problems—those problems that cut across all disciplinary boundaries. Philosophy needs to become again what it was for Socrates: the attempt to devote reason to the growth of wisdom in life.

18. Academic contributions need to be written in as simple, lucid, jargon-free a way as possible, so that academic work is as accessible as possible across specialities and to non-academics.

19. There needs to be a change in views about what constitute academic contributions, so that publications which promote (or have the potential to promote) public understanding as to what our problems of living are and what we need to do about them are included, in addition to contributions addressed primarily to the academic community.

20. Every university needs to create a seminar or symposium devoted to the sustained discussion of fundamental problems that cut across all conventional academic boundaries, global problems of living being included as well as global problems of knowledge and understanding.

The above changes all follow from the "from knowledge to wisdom" argument spelled out above. The following three institutional innovations do not follow from that argument but, if implemented, would help wisdom-inquiry to flourish.

21. Natural science needs to create committees, in the public eye, and manned by scientists and non-scientists alike, concerned to highlight and discuss failures of the priorities of research to respond to the interests of those whose needs are the greatest — the poor of the earth — as a result of the inevitable tendency of research priorities to reflect the interests of those who pay for science, and the interests of scientists themselves.

22. Every national university system needs to include a national shadow government, seeking to do, virtually, free of the constraints of power, what the actual national government ought to be doing. The hope would be that virtual and actual governments would learn from each other.

23. The world's universities need to include a virtual world government which seeks to do what an actual elected world government ought to do, if it existed. The virtual world government would also have the task of working out how an actual democratically elected world government might be created.[40]

Conclusion

Humanity is in deep trouble. We urgently need to learn how to make progress towards a wiser, more civilized world. This in turn requires that we possess traditions and institutions of learning rationally designed — *well designed* — to help us achieve this end. It is just this that we do not have at present. What we have instead is natural science and, more broadly, inquiry devoted to acquiring knowledge. Judged from the standpoint of helping us create a better world, knowledge-inquiry of this type is dangerously and damagingly irrational. We need to bring about a major intellectual and institutional revolution in the aims and methods of inquiry, from knowledge-inquiry to wisdom-inquiry. Almost every branch and aspect of academic inquiry needs to change.

A basic intellectual task of academic inquiry would be to articulate our problems of living (personal, social, and global) and propose and critically assess possible solutions, possible actions. This would be the task of social inquiry and the humanities. Tackling problems of knowledge would be secondary. Social inquiry would be at the heart of the academic enterprise, intellectually more fundamental than natural science. On a rather more long term basis, social inquiry would be concerned to help humanity build hierarchical methods of problem-solving into the fabric of social and political life so that we may gradually acquire the capacity to resolve our conflicts and problems of living in more cooperatively rational ways than at present. Natural science would change to include three domains of discussion: evidence, theory, and aims — the latter including discussion of metaphysics, values, and politics. Academia would actively seek to educate the public by means of discussion and debate, and would not just study the public.

This revolution — intellectual, institutional, and cultural — if it ever comes about, will be comparable in its long term impact to that of the Renaissance, the scientific revolution, or the Enlightenment. The outcome will be traditions and institutions of learning rationally designed to help us acquire wisdom. There are a few scattered signs that this intellectual revolution, from knowledge to wisdom, is already under way, as we shall see in chapter four. It will need, however, much wider cooperative support — from scientists, scholars, students, research councils, university administrators, vice chancellors, teachers, the media, government, and the general public — if it is to become anything more than what it is at present, a fragmentary and often impotent movement of protest and opposition, often at odds with itself, exercising little influence on the main body of academic work. I can hardly imagine any more important work for anyone associated with academia than, in teaching, learning, and research, to help promote this revolution.

Notes

1   For a much more detailed exposition of knowledge-inquiry, or "the philosophy of knowledge", see Maxwell (1984 or 2007a, ch. 2). For

evidence that knowledge-inquiry prevails in academia, see Maxwell (1984, ch. 6; 2000a; 2007a, ch. 6). I do not claim that everything in academia accords with the edicts of knowledge-inquiry. My claim is, rather, that this is the only candidate for rational inquiry in the public arena; it is the dominant view, exercising an all-pervasive influence over academe. Work that does not conform to its edicts has to struggle to survive.

2   For a more detailed characterization of wisdom see Maxwell (1984, p. 66; or 2007a, p. 79).

3   This assumption may be challenged. Does not academic inquiry seek knowledge for its own sake — it may be asked — whether it helps promote human welfare or not? Later on, I will argue that the conception of inquiry I am arguing for, wisdom-inquiry, does better justice than knowledge-inquiry to *both* aspects of inquiry, pure and applied. The basic aim of inquiry, according to wisdom-inquiry, is to help us realize what is of value in life, "realize" meaning both "apprehend" and "make real". "Realize" thus accommodates both aspects of inquiry, "pure" research or "knowledge pursued for its own sake" on the one hand, and technological or "mission-oriented" research on the other — both, ideally, seeking to contribute to what is of value in human life. Wisdom-inquiry, like sight, is there to help us find our way around. And, like sight, wisdom-inquiry is of value to us in two ways: for its intrinsic value, and for practical purposes. The first is almost more precious than the second.

4   For a more detailed development of this argument see Maxwell (1980; 1992; 2000a; 2004a; and especially 1984 or 2007a).

5   Funds devoted, in the USA, UK, and some other wealthy countries, to military research are especially disturbing: see Langley (2005) and Smith (2003).

6   See Maxwell (1984 or 2007a, ch. 3) for a much more detailed discussion of the damaging social repercussions of knowledge-inquiry.

7   This two-way interaction between science and society — a central feature of wisdom-inquiry as portrayed in Maxwell (1984) — is emphasized more recently by Nowotny *et al.* (2001).

8   Gay (1973).

9   See Aron (1968; 1970); Farganis (1993, Introduction); Hayek (1979).

10   The blunders of the *philosophes* are not entirely undetected. Karl Popper, in his first four works, makes substantial improvements to the traditional Enlightenment programme (although Popper does not himself present his work in this fashion). Popper first improves traditional conceptions of the progress-achieving methods of science (Popper, 1959). This improved conception, *falsificationism*, is then generalized to become *critical rationalism*. This is then applied to

social, political, and philosophical problems (Popper, 1961; 1962; 1963). The version of the Enlightenment programme about to be outlined here can be regarded as a radical improvement of Popper's version: see Maxwell (2004a, ch. 3; 2012a).

11 See d'Alembert (1963); Popper (1963).

12 In other words, T*, the empirically more successful rival to T, is just like T except that (a) T has been modified arbitrarily to yield predictions that differ from T for as yet unobserved phenomena, and (b) an independently testable and empirically confirmed hypothesis, H, has been added to T, H being about phenomena that lie beyond the scope of T. If T runs into empirical difficulties and is, ostensibly, refuted (as many accepted physical theories are), T* can be the outcome of modifying T arbitrarily so that it successfully predicts what refutes T. As a result, T* is, on the face of it, empirically more successful than T in that (a) T* successfully predicts phenomena that, ostensibly, refute T, (b) T* successfully predicts phenomena that lie beyond the scope of T, and (c) T* and T make different predictions about phenomena not yet observed. We can set out to refute T*, of course, but endlessly many more T*-type theories can always be concocted. In scientific practice, a theory like T* would never be considered for a moment, even though it is, on the face of it, empirically more successful than T, just because T* is grossly ad hoc and disunified. It is what may be called a "patchwork quilt" theory, in that it is made up of arbitrary bits and pieces stuck together, different laws applying to different phenomena.

13 More precisely: the universe is such that all *precise* disunified physical theories are false. If the universe is such that the true physical "theory of everything" is unified, there will be infinitely many true *imprecise* theories that are disunified.

14 Natural science has made such astonishing progress in improving knowledge and understanding of nature because it has put something like the hierarchical methodology, indicated here, into scientific practice. Officially, however, scientists continue to hold the standard empiricist view that no untestable metaphysical theses concerning the comprehensibility and knowability of the universe are accepted as a part of scientific knowledge. As I have argued elsewhere (Maxwell, 2004a, ch. 2), science would be even more successful, in a number of ways, if scientists adopted and explicitly implemented the hierarchical methodology indicated here.

15 For more detailed presentations of this argument see Maxwell (1998; 2002; 2004a, especially chs. 1, 2, and appendix; 2005a; 1984 or 2007a, chs. 5 and 9; 2011a). See also Maxwell (1974; 1993; 2008). My most recent, and perhaps my best, detailed exposition of the argument for

aim-oriented empiricism is to be found in Maxwell (2013). See also Maxwell (2007a, ch. 14).

[16] See Maxwell (1984 or 2007a, ch. 5; 2004a, pp. 51–67).

[17] One thinker who has stressed the inherently problematic, contradictory character of the idea of civilization is Isaiah Berlin; see, for example, Berlin (1980, pp. 74–9). Berlin thought the problem could not be solved; I, on the contrary, hold that the hierarchical methodology indicated here provides us with the means to learn how to improve our solution to it in real life. I return to the issue in chapter five.

[18] See Maxwell (1984, or 2007a, chs. 3, 6, and 7). See also Maxwell (2000a).

[19] The big contrast between social inquiry pursued within the contexts of knowledge-inquiry and wisdom-inquiry is that, whereas the former seeks to assess *theories* by means of experience, the latter seeks to assess *policies* by means of experience. Both are empirical; both appeal to experience. But whereas the former is concerned, in the first instance, to develop and assess *theories* about social phenomena (somewhat as theories about natural phenomena are developed and assessed in natural science), the latter seeks to develop and assess *policies, proposals for action, philosophies of life* that range from the highly specific to the general.

[20] Maxwell (1976a and 2nd ed., p. 5).

[21] See Snow (1986).

[22] For much more detailed arguments for wisdom-inquiry see Maxwell (1984 or 2007a). See also Maxwell (1976a; 2001; 2004a; 2010a). For summaries of the argument, see Maxwell (1980; 1992; 2000a; 2007b; 2008; 2009b; 2012a).

[23] Quoted in Hoffmann (1973, p. ix).

[24] Einstein (1973, p. 80).

[25] Einstein (1973, p. 11).

[26] Einstein (1949, p. 17).

[27] A recent, remarkable exception is Penrose (2004).

[28] For proposals as to how education might be conducted so as to encourage curiosity and problem-solving see Maxwell (2005b).

[29] These considerations are developed further in Maxwell (1976a; 1984 or 2007a; 2004a and 2010a). See also Maxwell (2012a).

[30] For a fuller exposition of such an account of empathic understanding see Maxwell (1984, pp. 171–89 and ch. 10, or 2007a, pp. 194–213 and ch. 10; and 2001, chs. 5–7 and 9).

[31] See Maxwell (1984, pp. 183–5, or 2007a, pp. 207–9).

[32] For more on this point see Maxwell (1998, chs. 4 and 8; 2004a, ch. 2).

[33] For a much fuller account of what is wrong with orthodox quantum

theory, its non-explanatory character, and what might be done to develop a better version of quantum theory, see Maxwell (1972; 1976b; 1982; 1994; 2004b; 2011b). Briefly, I argue that, in the 1920s and 1930s, arguments about quantum theory polarized into two camps: the Bohr/Heisenberg camp, which argued for the abandonment of realism and determinism, and the Einstein/Schrödinger camp, which argued for the retention of realism and determinism. As a result, no one pursued the most obvious option of retaining realism but abandoning determinism. It is this third, overlooked option that I have pursued. I have developed a fully micro-realistic, fundamentally probabilistic version of quantum theory which, if correct, solves the quantum wave/particle dilemma by holding that electrons, photons, atoms, etc. are a new kind of fundamentally probabilistic physical entity I call the *propensiton*. This version of quantum theory recaptures all the empirical success of the orthodox theory, is testably distinct from the orthodox theory, but has not yet been put to the test of experiment. The crucial experiments are difficult to perform.

[34]   See Ryle (1949, ch. II).

[35]   For a development of this point, see Maxwell (1984, pp. 174–81; 2007a, pp. 197–205).

[36]   For a more detailed discussion, see Maxwell (1984, pp. 59–63; or 2007a, pp. 72–5). That wisdom-inquiry is designed to promote cooperative rationality in life whereas knowledge-inquiry promotes mere manipulation is a theme that runs through much of my *From Knowledge to Wisdom* (1984 or 2007a).

[37]   The capacity of natural science, pursued solely to improve knowledge and understanding in a way that is unrelated to practical or technological problems, nevertheless to come up with results that have unanticipated, valuable practical applications.

[38]   See, for example, Popper (1961).

[39]   See Maxwell (2010b).

[40]   This is a modified version of the list to be found in Maxwell (2004a, pp. 119–21).

Chapter Three

How Wisdom-Inquiry Helps Solve Global Problems

Let us now suppose that a miracle has occurred. Stubborn academic conservatism, careerism, and dogmatism have been overcome, the quiet voice of reason has triumphed, and wisdom-inquiry now prevails in universities all around the globe. Would this really help us solve our immense global problems, and thus help us make progress towards as good a world as possible? How would this academic revolution make such a difference?

I begin by indicating ways in which differences between knowledge-inquiry and wisdom-inquiry are likely to have an impact on our capacity to solve our global problems and make progress towards a better world. I then consider, briefly, what we need to do to solve major global problems. I then go on to discuss how and why having wisdom-inquiry actively pursued in our universities round the world really would substantially help us do what we need to do to solve these problems. Wisdom-inquiry really would enable us to do what we seem incapable of doing today: progressively resolve the grave problems that confront us. We really would be able to make progress towards a world in which there is peace, justice, democracy, and sustainable prosperity. Finally, I consider objections.

Differences that Matter

Knowledge-inquiry can be of value to humanity in the following ways. It enhances our knowledge and understanding of aspects of the world around us, and ourselves; it develops new knowledge and technological know-how that enable us to achieve goals of value to us, having to do with health, prosperity, transport, communications, manufacturing, agriculture — the myriad goods of the modern world; and it educates students and trains professionals: doctors, engineers, lawyers, architects, teachers.

Wisdom-inquiry does all this too, but it does much in addition that knowledge-inquiry does not do.

(1) Wisdom-inquiry gives intellectual priority to the tasks of articulating problems of living and proposing and critically assessing possible solutions, possible actions, policies, political programmes, new institutional arrangements, philosophies of life, the aim being to discover those actions that are doable and such that, if performed, really do help us realize what is of value in life, and help us make progress towards as good a world as possible.

(2) Wisdom-inquiry actively engages with the public, the great social world beyond academia, in learning from, arguing with, and educating the public, government, industry, the media, and other centres of power and influence. Wisdom-inquiry does all it can to find those individuals and groups, whoever and wherever they may be, who have, in practice, in their lives, discovered new, valuable solutions to problems of living, so that what has been discovered may be communicated to others, and they may benefit too from what has been learned. Academia hunts out, in the social world, ideas, discoveries, arguments, innovations that have the capacity, if implemented, to help us realize what is of value in life — help us make progress towards a wiser world: it sucks them up, and broadcasts them, so that they may become generally available. Academics learn from non-academics, but also argue with, and seek to educate, non-

academics. Wisdom-inquiry engages in what may be termed rational politics; it does not manipulate or seek to persuade: it puts forward policies, ideas, and arguments for consideration. What matters, from the standpoint of wisdom-inquiry, is the quality of the thinking that goes on in the world that guides action. Academic thought is but a means to that end. Academia is humanity's institutional instrument, designed to help humanity learn how to live wisely. Knowledge-inquiry, by contrast, explicitly prohibits this kind of social engagement. The public are to be studied, not learned from and taught. Whereas knowledge-inquiry demands that one has a Ph.D. before one can contribute to academic thought, wisdom-inquiry makes no such demand. Wisdom-inquiry pounces on and broadcasts the very best ideas, wherever they are to be found.

(3) According to knowledge-inquiry, social inquiry tackles problems of knowledge about social phenomena; once acquired, this knowledge can be applied to help solve social problems. According to wisdom-inquiry, the primary task of social inquiry is to articulate problems of living and propose and criticize possible solutions—the pursuit of knowledge being a secondary matter.

(4) Natural science pursued within the framework of knowledge-inquiry puts standard empiricism into practice. This recognizes, broadly speaking, just two domains of scientific discussion: (i) evidence, and (ii) theory. Natural science, within the context of wisdom-inquiry, puts aim-oriented empiricism into practice and acknowledges a third vital domain of discussion, namely (iii) aims. Highly problematic metaphysical, value, and political assumptions are inherent in the aims, the priorities, of scientific research, and these need sustained imaginative and critical exploration, by scientists and non-scientists alike, to give us our best chances of improving research aims so that science may respond sensitively to the real needs and problems of humanity. The exploration of problems of living, conducted by social

inquiry, contributes to the task of choosing good aims for science.

(5) Social inquiry also has the task of getting into social life, into diverse social endeavours and institutions such as government, industry, finance, the media, international relations, the aim-improving meta-methods of aim-oriented rationality generalized from the progress-achieving methods of science of aim-oriented empiricism. All our current global problems are the outcome of failing to improve problematic aims of massively influential social endeavours, such as industry, agriculture, medicine, modern armaments, and the military — as we saw briefly in chapter one.

(6) A university that puts wisdom-inquiry into practice maintains a "Symposium", to which everyone is invited, from undergraduate to vice-chancellor, which keeps alive exploration of global problems, both intellectual and practical, the intention being that ideas discussed in the Symposium will influence (and be influenced by) more specialized research and education. Such a Symposium would help focus minds on what our problems of living are, and what we should do about them.

(7) Wisdom-inquiry, again, supports a shadow government which ponders problems facing the actual government free of the pressures of power, re-election, public opinion, the media, finance, powerful allies and enemies, to which actual governments are subject. It is reasonable to expect that the deliberations of such a shadow government would have a beneficial impact on public opinion, public debate, and actions of the actual government.

All these seven ways in which the two paradigms differ are such as to render wisdom-inquiry much more active and effective in helping humanity tackle successfully the immense global problems we face.

Five Global Problems: What We Need to Do

I now consider five global problems in turn: global warming, war, population growth, world poverty, and destruction of natural habitats and extinction of species. I indicate, in each case, in a rough and ready way, what needs to be done to solve the problems, and then go on to discuss how wisdom-inquiry could help, if put into practice by universities around the world.

Global Warming. This would seem to be the most serious of our problems. Let me state the obvious. In order to get to grips with this problem, the industrially advanced world needs to cut back on its emissions of CO_2 (carbon dioxide) as rapidly as possible. We must stop burning oil and coal, and rapidly develop alternative sources of power: wind, hydro-electric, wave, tidal, sunlight via photoelectric cells, biomass fuels, and, perhaps, nuclear power. Vehicles powered by petrol must be replaced by vehicles powered by batteries[1] (charged by electricity in turn produced by sustainable means that do not emit CO_2). Energy saving devices need to be installed in homes, offices, factories, and other buildings. Street lighting needs to be made more energy efficient. At the same time, global cooperation is required to put an end to the destruction of tropical rain forests, which significantly contributes to global warming.

Many of these measures are highly problematic, for both technical and social reasons. Wind power, hydro-electric power, and tidal power all tend to have adverse environmental consequences. Growing biomass fuels takes land away from the production of crops for much needed food. Nuclear power is, of course, notoriously problematic, in part because of the long-lasting, highly radioactive material that it produces, in part because of the link with nuclear weapons. Electric vehicles at present have nothing like the range or power of petrol or diesel fuelled vehicles. It is not clear what is to replace oil when it comes to ships and aeroplanes.

It may prove possible to harvest sunlight on an industrial scale by means of photo-electric panels spread over square miles in deserts. But photo-electric panels are expensive, and there are problems of transporting electricity to cities and densely populated areas — which tend to be far away from deserts. There are, however, at the time of writing, plans to create vast solar power stations in sun-drenched deserts and transport the electricity to centres of population.[2]

There are speculative ideas about how it might be possible to extract CO_2 from the atmosphere in sufficient quantities to make a difference, or to cut down on the amount of sunlight reaching the earth, for example by sending mirrors into space between us and the sun. All these ideas seem at present impractical, because of expense or adverse consequences or, quite simply, because they would not work.

The world needs to cooperate on putting a stop to the destruction of tropical rain forests. Countries such as Brazil and Indonesia need financial and other assistance from the industrially advanced world. Tropical rain forests require international policing to stop destructive logging.

The planet will continue to grow warmer even if we stopped all emissions of CO_2 overnight. This is because there is a delay in the planetary system. The CO_2 we have already put into the atmosphere will continue to turn up the heat for some time to come. As it is, of course, it will at best take decades for the world to reduce substantially its emissions of CO_2. Global warming will continue for decades to come. Low lying islands and coastal regions will have to be abandoned, as sea levels rise, and other regions will have to be abandoned because of heat and drought. As populations rise, land available for habitation and agriculture will shrink, not a good prospect for peace. World-wide cooperation will be needed to take care of refugees who come from regions made uninhabitable by global warming.

War. The world needs an international peace-keeping force which can be deployed swiftly anywhere on earth to intervene if violent conflict seems likely, or has already broken out, whether internal to a country or between nations. At present, the UN is supposed to perform this function, but does so ineffectually, partly because it cannot intervene in civil war, partly because the UN security council must reach agreement, and this is either not forthcoming at all, or only after a protracted period of wheeling and dealing. Sometimes the UN supports military intervention it ought not to support, as in the case of the Afghanistan war[3] after 9/11, while on other occasions it fails to support intervention it clearly ought to support, as in cases of conflict in Africa, in the former Yugoslavia, in Rwanda, and in Syria in 2011 and 2012.

It may well be that, in order to have an international peace-keeping force that does the job properly, we first need to establish a democratic, enlightened world government. That, it might be argued, rather puts the cart before the horse. We will only be able to establish a democratic world government if we have already established world peace. It seems reasonable to hold, however, that efforts to establish world peace should work in tandem with efforts to establish democratic world government.

More than an effective, humanitarian peace-keeping force is required to establish world peace, as the case of Europe graphically illustrates. For centuries, Europe suffered war after war, culminating in the horrors of the First and Second World Wars, both of which had their source in Europe. After the Second World War, a number of politicians and others worked hard to develop trade and other interconnections between European states so that all future European wars would be unthinkable. This hope has been fully realized. Yugoslavia does not really constitute an exception since that country was never a part of the efforts to create the Common Market, or the European Union. We have here something like a model for what we should try to create world-wide. For this to succeed, though, it will probably be necessary for there to be democracies in all the countries of the world, and far greater equality of wealth than at present around the world. (This proposal is very definitely not the view that the rest of the world should become European in character and culture; it is rather the view that something important is to be learned from the manner in which European peace has been established after centuries of war, for the establishment of peace throughout the rest of the world. We have here a particular example of what can be accomplished.)[4]

We require, too, a massive reduction in armaments and the military, all over the world, and especially in the USA and UK. All nuclear weapons need to be destroyed, there needs to be a nuclear inspection body, and the arms industry needs to be massively curtailed.

Population Growth. The world's population is predicted to rise to over 9 billion by 2050. Population growth adds to global warming, increases likelihood of war, undermines economic growth, and tends to speed up destruction of natural habitats, extinction of species, and over-fishing of the sea. One relatively cheap and practical measure that could be taken to slow down population growth would be to ensure that every woman on the planet of child bearing age has access to reliable birth control methods: the pill, the condom, the coil. It does not help that this is opposed by the Catholic Church, and was opposed by the Bush administration in the USA. One view is that population growth tends to level off as countries become wealthier. Parents tend not to have so many children—the argument goes—because the need to provide them with an education makes children more expensive, parents do not need to have children to care for them in old age because they can rely on state care, and falling death rates among children mean that it is no longer seen as essential to have lots of children to ensure that some survive. It is foolish to rely on these mechanisms, however, to slow down population growth. What is required is an effective programme world-wide to ensure that every woman of child bearing age has access to reliable contraception.

World Poverty. The debt of the poor countries of the world needs to be cancelled. There needs to be a change in world trading agreements, to ensure that it is the poor countries that are favoured, and not the rich. It must be permitted for poor countries to implement protectionism, to protect fledging industries against international competition. At the time of writing, wealthy countries control financial bodies in their own interests, bodies such as the IMF and World Bank. This needs to change.

A new global Marshall Plan needs to be created, funded by the wealthy countries of the world—the USA, Canada, Europe,

Japan, Australia, New Zealand, and perhaps others—to help poor countries develop in as sustainable a way as possible, the emphasis being on education and the development of appropriate industry and agriculture. This needs to be allied to efforts to promote democracy, and to put a stop to political corruption. More scientific and technological research needs to be devoted to the problems of the poor: problems of health, agriculture, communications, education, appropriate industrial development.

Destruction of Natural Habitats and Extinction of Species. As an integral part of the global Marshall Plan, indicated above, wealthy countries need to collaborate with poor and developing countries to take those measures required to stop the destruction of tropical rain forests and other natural habitats. This involves both deploying and adequately financing and equipping environmental police to put a stop to logging and hunting. It also involves providing aid for alternative, more sustainable methods of development. Agriculture needs to be developed in such a way that habitats remain for wildlife to flourish. There needs to be enhanced protection for endangered species.

I put these global policy proposals forward, not because I think they make a startlingly original contribution to thought about how we are to solve our global problems, but rather to indicate the kind of things we need to do to solve these problems. We need this as background to help answer the crucial question of the next section: "How would wisdom-inquiry help us put global policies such as these successfully into practice?"

I am well aware that some governments, many NGOs, the UN, social businesses, countless individuals and officials are already working hard to implement many aspects of these policies. Despite all these efforts, progress towards implementing the policies I have indicated (or better versions of these policies) remains agonizingly slow. Some of our global problems are intensifying—most notably global warming.

Some may complain that not enough detail has been given to assess these policy proposals. I have, however, I think, said enough for the purposes of the argument of the next section.

Others may complain that some, or even all, of what I have proposed is wrong-headed, and such that, if put into practice, would have dire consequences, the very opposite of what is intended. Those who believe in the universal efficacy of the free market to solve our problems are likely, in particular, to object to much of the above. My reply is that even if the above policies are misguided, in part or in total, this will not substantially affect the argument of the next section. It must be remembered that a basic task of wisdom-inquiry is (a) to articulate global problems, and (b) propose and critically assess possible solutions. Nothing is presupposed about what our problems are and what we need to do about them: wisdom-inquiry is intended to help enlighten us about these matters. Furthermore, even if we do need different policies from the above to solve our problems, nevertheless the argument of the next section goes through — as long as it is agreed that we need to tackle our problems *democratically*.

How Could Wisdom-Inquiry Help?

How exactly, it may be asked, could wisdom-inquiry help humanity implement these policies — if that is what is required — and thus help solve our global problems in a way which is so much more effective than knowledge-inquiry? Let us suppose that the academic revolution has occurred. Universities everywhere put wisdom-inquiry into practice. How could this make such a substantial difference to our capacity to solve global problems humanely and effectively, thus making progress towards as good a world as possible?

In essence, the answer is extremely simple. Our only hope of solving our global problems successfully lies with tackling these problems *democratically*. Benevolent, enlightened dictatorships or autocracies will not meet with success. But if democratic tackling of global problems is to succeed, we first need democracy to be established around the world, and second we need electorates — the world's population — to have an enlightened understanding of what our global problems are, and what we need to do about them. If this is lacking, democratic governments will not be able to implement the policies that are required. If, on the other hand, a majority of the world's people do have a good understanding of what our problems are, and what needs to be done about them, there is a good chance governments will respond to what this majority demands. This assumes, of course, that it is in the interests of the majority that global problems be solved. If this is not the case, then many might see clearly what needs to be done, but might nevertheless oppose the doing of it. I shall discuss this possibility in the next but one section.

A crucial requirement for tackling global problems successfully, then, is that a majority of the world's people have a good understanding of what these problems are, and what needs to be done about them. This is quite drastically lacking at present. Indeed, it may seem quite absurdly utopian to think it would ever be possible for most people on earth to agree about what our problems are, and what we need to do about them.

Step forward wisdom-inquiry. It is just here that wisdom-inquiry makes a dramatic difference. A basic task of wisdom-inquiry is (a) to articulate problems of living, including global problems, and (b) to propose and critically assess possible solutions—actual and possible actions, policies, political programmes, economic strategies, philosophies of life.[5]

A university that puts wisdom-inquiry into practice would hold a big Symposium once a month (let us say) devoted to discussing what our global problems are, and how they are to be solved. Everyone at the university would be invited to attend and participate, from undergraduate to professor and vice-chancellor. The Symposium might sometimes be big affairs, involving the media, with well-known speakers, while on other occasions it might be smaller, more private, an affair for a group of specialists, devoted to some specific issue. The aim would be not just to highlight existing problems, or criticize existing policies, but to come up with workable, realistic, effective new policies. The constitution of the university would be such that good ideas developed in the Symposium would be capable of influencing more specialized research in the university, and would be critically assessed by such research. One result of the Symposium would be that all those associated with, and educated in, universities, from professor to undergraduate, would acquire a good understanding of what our global problems are, what is and is not being done about them, what could be done, and what kind of research and education is required to help solve them. A long term task of social inquiry would be to help build aim-oriented rationality into our diverse institutions — government, industry, finance, agriculture, international trade, the military, the media, the law, education — so that problematic aims may be transformed to become those that help solve global problems. A fundamental task for universities implementing wisdom-inquiry is to educate the public about what our global problems are, and what we need to do about them. This would be done, not by *instruction*, but by lively discussion and debate; ideas, arguments, and information flowing in both directions. There would be powerful inducements for academics to engage in public education by means of public discussion and lectures, articles in newspapers, popular books, broadcasts, blogs on the internet, even novels and plays. All academics want to make a contribution to academic thought, not only for its own sake, but also because this leads to academic status and prestige, academic prizes, and career advancement. Granted wisdom-inquiry, contributions are judged in terms of their capacity to help people realize what is of value in life. Working within the framework of wisdom-inquiry, academics would be highly motivated, in other words, to engage in the kind of public education I have indicated (since this is integral to what counts as an academic contribution). A central purpose of academia would be to promote cooperatively rational tackling of problems of living in the social world, and put aim-oriented rationality into practice in personal and social life. The problematic aims and priorities of scientific and technological research would be subjected to sustained, imaginative exploration and criticism, by academics and non-academics alike, this feeding into, and making use of, the discussion of problems of living going on within and without academia. Wisdom-inquiry is designed to engage in rational discussion of political policies and programmes, and to promote this as well. Universities would have just sufficient power to retain their independence from pressures of government, public opinion, industry, and the media, but no more. It would be standard for a nation's universities to include a shadow government. If the actual government does not permit such a thing, universities would clamour to be free to create it and, in doing so, would receive international support. The nation's university shadow government would be entirely without power, but would also be free of all the constraints and pressures that actual power is subject to, which tend to distort and corrupt what actual governments do. The shadow university government would seek to develop and publish ideal possible actions, policies, and legislative programmes which the nation's actual government ought to be developing and enacting. The idea would be that learning would go on in both directions, the ideal university shadow government learning about the realities of power, the nation's actual government learning to distinguish what is merely politically expedient from what is in the interests of the nation and humanity, a fund of good ideas for policies and legislation being readily available from the shadow government. Finally, the world's universities would contain a shadow university world government which would do, for the world, what national shadow governments do for nations. A basic task would be to work out how an actual world government might be created, what form this should take, what its desirable and undesirable consequences would be likely to be.

In brief, the whole character, structure, activity, aims, and ideals of wisdom-inquiry universities would be such as to be devoted to helping humanity learn how to resolve global problems in increasingly cooperatively rational ways, thus making increasingly assured progress towards as good a world as possible. Universities would be humanity's means to learn how to create a genuinely civilized world.

The contrast with knowledge-inquiry is devastating. Knowledge-inquiry fails to do almost everything that needs to be done to help humanity make progress in tackling global problems. Knowledge-inquiry does, it is true, acquire knowledge and technological know-how, and make this available, primarily to government agencies and industry, to be used to solve practical problems. This can undeniably be of great value and, as we have seen, has made possible the creation of the modern world. But almost everything else that needs to be done is rigorously excluded from the intellectual domain of academia under the misguided idea that this is necessary to preserve the objectivity and reliability, the authentically factual character, of the knowledge that is acquired. Far from giving priority to (a) articulating global problems, and (b) proposing and critically assessing possible solutions, these vital intellectual activities are excluded from knowledge-inquiry altogether, on the grounds that they involve politics, values, action, human suffering, morality, and can only undermine, and not contribute to, the pursuit of factual knowledge. Again, far from giving priority to the task of introducing aim-oriented rationality into the social world, knowledge-inquiry does not even put aim-oriented rationality into practice *itself*, in science, social inquiry, or the humanities. There is no place for the Symposium devoted to tackling global problems. Social science and the humanities seek to improve knowledge and understanding of social and cultural phenomena, but do not actively try to transform social life. Individual academics may take it upon themselves to contribute to public education but this is, as it were, an extra-curriculum activity, not a part of the official business of professional academic life—which is to contribute to the growth of knowledge. Far from academia encouraging discussion and debate with the public, ideas being encouraged to flow in both directions, knowledge-inquiry, quite to the contrary, demands that the intellectual domain of inquiry be sealed off from the corrupting influence of the social world, so that only those considerations relevant to the acquisition of knowledge of truth may influence what is accepted and rejected, such as evidence and valid argument. Knowledge-inquiry provides every inducement to academics to seek to contribute to knowledge, but no inducement whatsoever to engage in the extra-curriculum activity of public education (since this does not contribute to knowledge). What matters is how well-established and significant a contribution to knowledge is, not whether it does, or does not, help enhance the quality of human life. The intellectual standards of knowledge-inquiry are almost exclusively concerned with the problem of distinguishing authentic contributions to knowledge from would-be contributions that fail to pass muster, in one way or another. These standards are not concerned to help improve the aims and priorities of research. Choosing what research aims receive financial support, and what do not, is left to research funding bodies to decide: it is not thrown open to sustained scientific and public discussion and debate. Inevitably, as a result, research priorities come to reflect the interests of those who do science, and those who pay for it — government and industry — rather than the interests of those whose needs are the greatest, the poor of the earth who, being poor, do not have the means to pay for scientific research. Vast sums are spent on military research, very little in comparison on research related to the diseases and problems of the poor of Africa, South America, and Asia. Finally, there can be no place for a shadow government in the university, granted knowledge-inquiry. Politics is to be excluded altogether from the intellectual domain of inquiry; only the pursuit of knowledge about political life is permitted.

The outcome of this wholesale failure to do what most needs to be done, apart from acquire knowledge, is just what might be expected. Much knowledge is acquired but this, in the absence of a more fundamental concern to help humanity solve global problems, does as much harm as good. Knowledge-inquiry, *instead of helping to solve global problems, helps to create and intensify them,* as we have seen.

I have concentrated on *universities*. But if the revolution were to occur in universities, it would have an impact throughout the whole educational and research world, as well as influencing dramatically, as I have tried to indicate, the media, government, the arts, the law, industry, agriculture, international relations, and personal and social life quite generally.

Changing knowledge-inquiry into wisdom-inquiry in universities throughout the civilized world would make a dramatic difference to the capacity of humanity to tackle global problems successfully.

Objections

Objection 1: Academics would never agree to put wisdom-inquiry into practice.

Reply: The arguments for the greater rationality, intellectual integrity, and potential human value of wisdom-inquiry are overwhelming. Once these arguments have been understood by a sufficient number of influential academics, funding bodies, and university administrators, universities will begin to move piecemeal towards wisdom-inquiry. Indeed, as I shall show in the next chapter, this academic transformation is, to some extent, already underway.

Objection 2: Governments, industry, public opinion would never permit the required academic revolution to take place.

Reply: Undoubtedly in some parts of the world today it would indeed be impossible. There would be difficulties in North Korea, Burma, Zimbabwe, Saudi Arabia, Iran, and even China and Russia. Even in the 30 full democracies of the world,[6] serious attempts to instigate wisdom-inquiry would meet with opposition. Even democratically elected governments are unlikely to take kindly to academic criticism of their policies, and to the creation of academic shadow governments. Those universities that took a lead in implementing wisdom-inquiry might find they were being penalized by having government funding decreased. Industry might withdraw funds as well. Academia would have an incredibly powerful argument in its hands to combat such manoeuvres: the changes are needed in the interests of rationality, intellectual integrity, and the future of humanity. The public could be alerted to the scandal of government attempting to suppress academic thought devoted to helping humanity make progress towards as good a world as possible. This objection does not look very plausible when one takes into account that the academic revolution, from knowledge to wisdom, is already underway to some extent, in the UK and elsewhere, as we shall see in the next chapter.

Objection 3: Even if the academic revolution occurred, it would have little impact, either because academics failed to agree among themselves, or because they are ignored by centres of power and influence.

Reply: We encountered a version of this objection in chapter one. A nightmare possibility is indeed that wisdom-inquiry academics simply reproduce all the standard ideas, prejudices, and disagreements of the social world around them. In the US, academics supporting the Democrats might slug it out with those supporting the Republicans, and no one learns anything. I acknowledge that this is a possibility, but it would betray the fundamental intellectual ideals of wisdom-inquiry. Those engaged in social inquiry need to treat policy ideas in a way that is analogous, in important respects, to the way natural scientists treat scientific theories: some such ideas may be hopeless, others may be partly good, partly bad, none is likely to be entirely good and sound. The all-important point is to pick out the best idea from its rivals, and subject it and its rivals to sustained critical examination, taking experience into account where possible, and if a better idea emerges from the pool of rivals, that should be adopted instead. It is of course just this that aim-oriented rationality is designed to facilitate, in the field of ideas for solutions to problems of living, on analogy with what aim-oriented empiricism facilitates within natural science. It will, for many reasons, be more difficult to protect wisdom-inquiry social thought from subversion than it is to protect natural science from subversion. Policy ideas are implicated in our lives, passions, ideals, and values directly, and are much harder to assess rationally and by means of experience than are scientific ideas. Experiments in the social world cannot be conducted freely in the way in which scientific experiments can.

As for academia being ignored even if it comes up with excellent, agreed ideas this, to some extent, is almost bound to occur. But only to some extent, and for a time. It took scientists decades to get governments, industry, the media, and the public to take global warming seriously. The long-standing failure to get the message across has finally led scientists to make changes to the nature of science—nudging things towards wisdom-inquiry, as we shall see in the next chapter. But finally, at the time of writing (2012), the message has been delivered although there are few signs, as yet, that much is being done to reduce CO_2 emissions in response to this message. In my view, the global warming message would have been communicated two or three decades earlier if wisdom-inquiry had been in place by 1945, let us say. The academic revolution we are considering would undoubtedly have a major impact, in the ways I have indicated, even if this impact would not be felt overnight, but would take a decade or so to filter through the intricacies of the social world.

Objection 4: Even if the academic revolution occurred, even if it came up with excellent policies and technologies, and even if these were appreciated and understood by governments and public alike, still this would not make much difference because the barrier to solving global problems is not lack of knowledge and understanding, but the unwillingness of the wealthy to make the necessary sacrifices. Too many wealthy, powerful people do not want to do what needs to be done.

Reply: The policies I have indicated above would undoubtedly meet with resistance, were they ever to be seriously on the political agenda. In the USA, for example, business corporations are very good at protecting what they see as their interests by lobbying, by funding sympathetic politicians and political parties, and by manipulating the media.[7] Even here, however, wisdom-inquiry could be effective, in that the public needs to become more enlightened about what these strategies are, and what needs to be done to combat them. This assumes that it is primarily the business and financial world which would want to oppose the policies we require. It could be argued that a majority of people living in wealthy countries do not want to support measures required to deal with global warming, or world poverty, because of the sacrifices that would have to be made. This, I believe, overestimates the sacrifices that are required, and underestimates concern people have for the future of the world. If policies are widely understood to be necessary, and likely to be effective, in tackling global warming, for example, or world poverty, then I believe a majority of people in wealthy countries would be willing to endorse these policies, even if some sacrifice is required. Why should a global Marshall Plan today meet with so much more resistance than the original Marshall Plan encountered when first instigated after the Second World War, when the USA was not as wealthy as it is today?

Conclusion

The basic point is extremely simple. If we are to make better progress towards as good a world as possible, we need to learn how to do it. That in turn requires that we have in our hands institutions of learning rationally devoted to that task. It is just this that we do not have at present — although there are hints that such institutions might be struggling to be born. What we have at present is academic inquiry devoted to the pursuit of knowledge which, as we have seen, helps create as many problems as it solves. We urgently need to transform our universities so that they come to put wisdom-inquiry into practice.

Notes

[1]   Vehicles powered by hydrogen are a possible alternative — hydrogen in turn produced by electricity produced by power stations that do not emit CO_2.

[2]   See for example www.desertec.org/ (accessed 8 May 2012).

[3]   9/11 was a monstrous crime, not an act of war, and could not conceivably justify war in retaliation. The UN issued a resolution which in effect supported the USA in its subsequent invasion of Afghanistan. It did so, in my view, because the aggrieved nation was the USA. If, instead, France had been the victim, the Louvre being destroyed in an analogous terrorist attack with, we may suppose, a similar loss of life (around 3,000 people), I feel sure the UN would not have supported France in a retaliatory invasion of Afghanistan.

[4]   At the time of writing, 2012, the European project is suffering a serious setback due to recession and serious doubts about the Euro (the

European currency). But even if the Euro disintegrates, it does not seem likely that this would lead to war among European nations. There is here, nevertheless, a dreadful warning for all plans designed to bring nations closer together into trading, financial, and political union.

5   Even if the policies I have outlined are the best available, they need to be developed in far greater detail before they qualify even for serious consideration. The chances are, of course, that some of what I have proposed deserves to be rejected, because it is unworkable, undesirable, or both.

6   *The Economist* has recently assessed the democratic character of the countries of the world: see http://en.wikipedia.org/wiki/Democracy_Index. There are 51 dictatorships, with North Korea at the bottom of the list.

7   See Goldenberg (2013).

Chapter Four

Is the Wisdom Revolution Underway?

So far I have drawn a stark contrast between knowledge-inquiry and wisdom-inquiry, and have suggested that knowledge-inquiry is at present dominant in universities all over the world. But is this really the case?

I have no doubt that it was the case 30 years ago. In 1983, for the first edition of my book *From Knowledge to Wisdom,* I investigated six relevant aspects of academia to see which conception of inquiry prevailed, and found that knowledge-inquiry was overwhelmingly dominant.[1] However, more recently, in 2003, I repeated the survey for the second edition of the book, and found that some changes had taken place in the direction of wisdom-inquiry, although knowledge-inquiry still dominated.[2] Since 2003, there have been further developments that have nudged some universities in the direction of wisdom-inquiry.

It is possible that the academic revolution really is underway, and we are in the middle of a dramatic transition from knowledge-inquiry to wisdom-inquiry. I now indicate some developments that have taken place during the last twenty years, in the main in universities in the UK, which can, perhaps, be interpreted as constituting steps towards wisdom-inquiry.[3]

Perhaps the most significant steps towards wisdom-inquiry that have taken place during the last twenty years are the creation of departments, institutions, and research centres concerned with social policy, with problems of environmental degradation, climate change, poverty, injustice, and war, and with such matters as medical ethics and community health.[4]

At Cambridge University there is a more interesting development. One can see the first hints of the institutional structure of wisdom-inquiry being superimposed upon the existing structure of knowledge-inquiry. As I have indicated, wisdom-inquiry puts the intellectual tackling of problems of living at the heart of academic inquiry, this activity being conducted in such a way that it both influences, and is influenced by, more specialized research. Knowledge-inquiry, by contrast, organizes intellectual activity into the conventional departments of knowledge: physics, chemistry, biology, history, and the rest, in turn subdivided, again and again, into ever more narrow, specialized research disciplines. But this knowledge-inquiry structure of ever more specialized research is hopelessly inappropriate when it comes to tackling our major problems of living. In order to tackle environmental problems, for example, in a rational and effective way, specialized research into a multitude of different fields, from geology, engineering, and economics to climate science, biology, architecture, and metallurgy, needs to be connected to, and coordinated with, the different aspects of environmental problems. The sheer urgency of environmental problems has, it seems, forced Cambridge University to create the beginnings of wisdom-inquiry organization to deal with the issue. The "Cambridge Environmental Initiative" (CEI), launched in December 2004, distinguishes eight fields associated with environmental problems: built environment; climate change; conservation; energy; natural hazards; society, policy, and law; waste; and water. Under these headings, it helps to coordinate the research of some 159 people working on specialized aspects of environmental issues in some 35 different (knowledge-inquiry) departments.[5]

The CEI holds seminars, workshops, and public lectures to put specialized research workers in diverse fields in touch with one another, and to inform the public.

A similar coordinating, interdisciplinary initiative exists at Oxford University. This is the School of Geography and the Environment, founded in 2005 under another name. This is made up of five research "clusters", two previously established research centres, the Environmental Change Institute (founded in 1991) and the Transport Studies Institute, and three inter-departmental research programmes, the African Environments Programme, the Oxford Water Futures Programme, and the Oxford branch of the Tyndall Centre (see below). The School also hosts a number of other research projects, including the Oxford Centre for Tropical Forests, and UKCIP which helps organizations to adapt to climate change.[6]

At Oxford University there is also the Oxford Martin School, founded in 2005 to "formulate new concepts, policies and tech-nologies that will make the future a better place to be". It is made up of over thirty interdisciplinary research teams based in Oxford University departments, and carries out research that ranges from ageing, armed conflict, cancer therapy, and carbon reduction to nanoscience, oceans, science innovation and society, the future of the mind, and the future of humanity. At Oxford there is also the Smith School of Enterprise and the Environment, founded in 2008 to help government and indus-try tackle the challenges of the 21st century, especially those associated with climate change.

Somewhat similar developments have taken place recently at my own university, University College London. Not only are there 141 research institutes and centres at UCL, some only recently founded, many interdisciplinary in character, devoted to such themes as ageing, cancer, cities, culture, public policy, the environment, global health, governance, migration, neuro-science, and security. In addition, in 2008, under the heading "UCL Grand Challenges",[7] David Price, vice-provost for research at UCL, has been instrumental in creating four broad areas of research—global health, sustainable cities, human well-being, intercultural interaction—which bring together special-ists from diverse fields to develop ideas, techniques, and poli-cies capable of helping humanity tackle our current grave global problems. UCL now seeks to implement "The Wisdom Agenda",[8] and is actively engaged in "Developing a culture of wisdom at UCL".[9] On its website, under the heading Grand Challenges, UCL puts the matter like this:

> The world is in crisis. Billions of us suffer from illness and disease, despite applicable preventions and cures. Life in our cities is under threat from dysfunctionality and climate change. The prospect of global peace and cooperation remains under assault from tensions between our nations, faiths and cultures. Our quality of life — actual and perceived — diminishes despite technological advances. These are global problems, and we must resolve them if future generations are to be provided with the opportunity to flourish.

These developments, surely echoed in many universities around the world, can be regarded as first steps towards implementing wisdom-inquiry.

Impressive too is the John Tyndall Centre for Climate Change Research, founded by 28 scientists from 10 different universities or institutions in 2000. It is based in eight British universities (Universities of East Anglia, Cardiff, Newcastle, Cambridge, Manchester, Oxford, Sussex, and Southampton), and Fudan University, Shanghai, China. The Centre says, "We bring together scientists, economists, engineers and social scientists who are working to develop sustainable responses to climate change. We work not just within the research community, but also with business leaders, policy advisors, the media and the public in general".[10] All this is strikingly in accordance with basic features of wisdom-inquiry.[11] We have here, perhaps, the real beginnings of wisdom-inquiry being put into academic practice.

A similar organization, modelled on the Tyndall Centre, is the UK Energy Research Centre (UKERC), launched in 2004. It says it "carries out world-class research into sustainable future energy systems. It is the hub of UK energy research and the gateway between the UK and the international energy research communities. Our interdisciplinary, whole systems research informs UK policy development and research strategy".[12]

UKERC coordinates research in a number of British universities and research institutions, and "participates and leads energy research activities internationally". It has created the National Energy Research Network (NERN), which seeks to link up the entire energy community, including people from academia, government, NGOs, and business.

Another possible indication of a modest step towards wisdom-inquiry is the growth of peace studies and conflict resolution research. In Britain, the Peace Studies Department at Bradford University has "quadrupled in size" since 1984 (Professor Paul Rogers, personal communication), and is now the largest university department in this field in the world. INCORE, an International Conflict Research project, was established in 1993 at the University of Ulster, in Northern Ireland, in conjunction with the United Nations University. It develops conflict resolution strategies, and aims to influence policymakers and others involved in conflict resolution. Like the newly created environmental institutions just considered, it is highly interdisciplinary in character, in that it coordinates work done in history, policy studies, politics, international affairs, sociology, geography, architecture, communications, and social work as well as in peace and conflict studies. The Oxford Research Group, established in 1982, is an independent think tank which seeks to develop "sustainable approaches to security as an alternative to violent global confrontation, through original research, wide-ranging dialogue, and practical policy recommendations".[13] It has links with a number of universities in Britain. Peace studies have also grown during the period we are considering at Sussex University, Kings College London, Leeds University, Lancaster University, Coventry University, and London Metropolitan University. Centres in this field in Britain created since 1984 include: the Centre for Peace and Reconciliation Studies at Warwick University founded in 1999; the Desmond Tutu Centre for War and Peace, established in 2004 at Liverpool Hope University; the Praxis Centre at Leeds Metropolitan University, launched in 2004; the Crime and Conflict Centre at Middlesex University; and the International

Boundaries Research Unit, founded in 1989 at Durham University.[14]

Additional indications of a general movement towards aspects of wisdom-inquiry are the following. Demos, a British independent think tank has, in recent years, convened conferences on the need for more public participation in discussion about aims and priorities of scientific research, and greater openness of science to the public.[15] This has been taken up by the Royal Society which, in 2004, published a report on potential benefits and hazards of nanotechnology produced by a group consisting of both scientists and non-scientists. The Royal Society also created a "Science in Society Programme" in 2000, with the aims of promoting "dialogue with society", of involving "society positively in influencing and sharing responsibility for policy on scientific matters", and of embracing "a culture of openness in decision-making" which takes into account "the values and attitudes of the public". A similar initiative is the "science in society" research programme funded by the Economic and Social Research Council which has, in the autumn of 2007, come up with six booklets reporting on various aspects of the relationship between science and society. Increasingly, scientists appreciate that engagement with the public is a vital part of the scientific enterprise. Many appreciate that non-scientists ought to contribute to discussion concerning science policy. There is a growing awareness among scientists and others of the role that values play in science policy, and the importance of subjecting medical and other scientific research to ethical assessment. That universities are becoming increasingly concerned about these issues is indicated by the creation, in recent years, of many departments of "science, technology, and society", in the UK, the USA, and elsewhere, the intention being that these departments will concern themselves with interactions between science and society.

Even though academia is not organized in such a way as to give intellectual priority to helping humanity tackle its current global problems, academics do nevertheless, of course, publish books that tackle these issues, for experts and non-experts alike.

For example, in recent years many books have been published on global warming and what to do about it.[16]

Here are a few further scattered hints that the wisdom-inquiry revolution may be underway — as yet unrecognized and unorganized. In recent years, research in psychology into the nature of wisdom has flourished, in the USA, Canada, Germany, and elsewhere.[17] Emerging out of this, and associated in part with Robert Sternberg, there is, in the USA, a "teaching for wisdom" initiative, the idea being that, whatever else is taught — science, history, or mathematics — the teaching should be conducted in such a way that wisdom is also acquired.[18] There is the Arete Initiative at Chicago University which recently "launched a $2 million research program on the nature and benefits of wisdom".[19] The "Defining Wisdom" website includes a long list of publications on wisdom since 1990, and provides information about 1,499 people who have signed up to the wisdom research network.[20]

There are two initiatives that I have been involved with personally. The first is a new international group of 347 scholars and educationalists called Friends of Wisdom, "an association of people sympathetic to the idea that academic inquiry should help humanity acquire more wisdom by rational means".[21] The second is a special issue of the journal *London Review of Education*; of which I was guest editor, devoted to the theme "wisdom in the university". This duly appeared in June 2007 (vol. 5, no. 2). It contains seven articles on various aspects of the basic theme.[22] Rather strikingly, another academic journal brought out a special issue on a similar theme in the same month. The April–June 2007 issue of *Social Epistemology* is devoted to the theme "wisdom in management" (vol. 21, no. 2). On 5 December 2007, *History and Policy* was launched, a new initiative that seeks to bring together historians, politicians, and the media, and "works for better public policy through an understanding of history".[23]

Out of curiosity, on 18 May 2009, I consulted Google, in connection with a number of relevant topics, to see whether the number of "results" might give some indication of whether the wisdom revolution is underway. I did the same thing over two years later, on 4 December 2011. Here are the results.

Topic	18 May 2009	6 December 2011
"Environmental Studies"	9,910,000	10,400,000
"Development Studies"	7,210,000	6,760,000
"Peace Studies"	529,000	2,070,000
"Policy Studies"	2,160,000	6,530,000
"Science, Technology, and Society"	297,000	1,090,000
"Wisdom Studies"	5,510	56,400
"From Knowledge to Wisdom"	18,100	68,500
"Wisdom-Inquiry"	625	7,340

These figures do not, perhaps, in themselves tell us very much. There is probably a great deal of repetition — and Google gives us no idea of the intellectual quality of the departments or studies that are being referred to.

One of the items that comes up in a Google search is Copthorne Macdonald's "The Wisdom Page" — a compilation of "various on-line texts concerning wisdom, references to books about wisdom, information about organizations that promote wisdom", and including bibliographies of more than 800 works on wisdom prepared by Richard Trowbridge.[24] The Stanford online Encyclopedia of Philosophy has had an entry on wisdom since 2007 (but only because I suggested to the editors that they ought to have one).[25] The online Wikiversity has a course on wisdom.[26] Perhaps wisdom-inquiry will develop first outside universities, and will only gradually percolate into universities as they are shamed into paying attention. This has happened before. Modern science began outside universities, and so too, later, social science. In February 2011 I attended a two-day conference on "transition universities" which took much of its inspiration and impetus from the "transition towns" movement.[27] The mood of the meeting, overwhelmingly, was that universities need to change dramatically if they are to help individuals and communities cope with the problems the future has in store for us.[28] The idea that universities have sold out to powerful interest groups and do not respond to the problems and aspirations of most people — it being necessary to create a people's university outside the university — seems to be held by many taking part in the "occupy movement" which began with "occupy Wall Street" in September 2011, and subsequently spread around the world. Writing in *The Guardian* in November 2011, this is what one participant had to say about "Tent City University" outside St. Paul's, in London.

> Over the past month, Tent City University has hosted speakers ranging from world-renowned academics to migrant cleaners fighting for the right to organise. We have attracted huge crowds to our events and steadily had almost eight hours pro-grammed every single day since we set up... Many have des-cribed us as an alternative to university, often positioning us in opposition to the limited range of ideas and exorbitant fees that characterise much contemporary higher education... But we are not merely an alternative; we are a direct challenge to the con-temporary structure of mainstream universities. In the neolib-eral era, the role of the university has been clear: to reproduce society with all its injustices, disenfranchisements and griev-ances.[29]

None of these developments quite amounts to wisdom-inquiry. One has to remember that "wisdom studies" is not the same thing as "wisdom-inquiry". The new environmental research organizations, and the new emphasis on policy studies of vari-ous kinds, do not in themselves add up to wisdom-inquiry. In order to put wisdom-inquiry fully into academic practice, it would be essential for social inquiry and the humanities to give far greater emphasis to the task of helping humanity learn how to tackle its immense global problems in more cooperatively rational ways than at present. The imaginative and critical exploration of problems of living would need to proceed at the heart of academia, in such a way that it influences science pol-icy, and is in turn influenced by the results of scientific and tech-nological research. Academia would need to give much more emphasis to public education by means of discussion and debate, ideas and arguments going in both directions. Our only hope of tackling global problems of climate change, poverty, war, and terrorism humanely and effectively is to tackle them democratically. But democratic governments are not likely to be all that much more enlightened than their electorates. This in turn means that electorates of democracies must have a good understanding of what our global problems are, and what needs to be done about them. Without that there is little hope of humanity making progress towards a better world. A vital task for universities is to help educate the public — and be educated by the public — about what we need to do to avoid — at the least — the worst of future possible disasters. Wisdom-inquiry would undertake such a task of public education to an extent that is far beyond anything attempted or imagined by academics today. There is still a long way to go before we have what we so urgently need, a kind of academic inquiry rationally devoted to helping humanity learn how to create a better world. A university system that did that would need, for example, to create a shadow government, creating policies and possible legislation, imaginatively and critically, free of the shackles actual governments suffer from because of all sorts of pressures, honourable and dishonourable. As far as I know, there is not at present even a hint of an awareness that such an institution needs to be created within academia.

Nevertheless, the developments I have indicated can be regarded as signs that there is a growing awareness of the need for our universities to change so as to help individuals learn how to realize what is genuinely of value in life — and help humanity learn how to tackle its immense global problems in wiser, more cooperatively rational ways than we seem to be doing at present. My calls for this intellectual and institutional revolution may so far have been in vain. But what I have been calling for, all these years, is perhaps, at last, beginning to happen, independently of my ineffective shouting on the sidelines. If so, it is happening with agonizing slowness, in a dreadfully muddled and piecemeal way. It urgently needs academics and non-academics alike to wake up to what is going on — or what needs to go on — to help give direction, coherence, and a rationale to this nascent revolution from knowledge to wisdom.

Notes

1   See my (1984, ch. 6).
2   See my (2007a, ch. 6).
3   What follows is adapted from my (2009a).
4   For more on this point, see Iredale (2007); and Macdonald (2009).
5   See www.cei.cam.ac.uk/ (accessed 2 December 2011).
6   See www.geog.ox.ac.uk/ (accessed 4 December 2011).
7   See www.ucl.ac.uk/grand-challenges/ (accessed 5 December 2011).
8   www.ucl.ac.uk/research/wisdom-agenda (accessed 5 December 2011).
9   The title of a policy document which can be downloaded from the UCL website: see www.ucl.ac.uk/research/wisdom-agenda/2011-UCL_Wisdom-Agenda.pdf. There is here, I confess, an input from my own work. For an interview I conducted with David Price and his team about their work, see Maxwell (2012b).
10   www.tyndall.ac.uk/about (accessed 5 December 2011).
11   Tyndall Centre, ed., *Truly Useful* (UK, Tyndall Centre).
12   www.ukerc.ac.uk/ (accessed 6 December 2011, as are the websites referred to below).
13   www.oxfordresearchgroup.org.uk/.
14   For an account of the birth and growth of peace studies in universities, see Rogers (2006).
15   See Wilson and Willis (2004).
16   See www.kings.cam.ac.uk/assets/d/da/Global_Warming_bibliography.pdf.
17   See, for example, Sternberg (1990).
18   See Sternberg *et al.* (2007).
19   See see http://wisdomresearch.org/.
20   http://wisdomresearch.org/Arete/UserList.aspx.
21   www.knowledgetowisdom.org.
22   Subsequently republished as a book: Barnett and Maxwell (2008).
23   www.historyandpolicy.org/.
24   www.wisdompage.com/.
25   http://plato.stanford.edu/entries/wisdom/.
26   http://en.wikiversity.org/wiki/Wisdom/Curriculum.
27   www.transitionnetwork.org/.
28   www.transitionuniversities.org.uk/.
29   Howard (2011).

Chapter Five

Policies for a Wiser World

As we move from knowledge-inquiry to wisdom-inquiry, changes need to be made to natural and technological science, to the relationship between these and social inquiry and the humanities, and to the relationship between academic inquiry as a whole and the rest of the social world. But the most radical changes that need to be made are to social science and the humanities. These cease to be devoted, primarily, to the pursuit of knowledge and understanding, and become centrally concerned to help humanity solve its conflicts and problems of living in more peaceful, just, fruitful, cooperatively rational ways. The task is, quite directly, to help humanity make progress towards a wiser world by intellectual and educational means.

Is it sufficient to reform social science and the humanities, or is something more radical required in order to put wisdom-inquiry into practice in universities? In this final chapter I attempt to sketch the changes that will need to be made to enable wisdom-inquiry to be put intelligently and effectively into academic practice.

The primary goal, let me re-emphasize, is to create a wiser world. Transforming the academic world is a means to that end.

I must acknowledge at the outset that social science does already, to some extent, do the kind of work I argue it ought to do. Universities do already engage in peace, policy, development, and environmental studies—as we saw in the last chapter. There are economists concerned about problems of well-being and happiness. Others study problems that arise as a result of migration, crime, poverty, loneliness, unemployment. There are philosophers concerned about the way we treat animals, biologists actively trying to help prevent destruction of natural habitats and extinction of species.

Overwhelmingly, nevertheless, social inquiry is at present pursued as social *science*, or at least as the pursuit of *knowledge* of social phenomena, within the framework of knowledge-inquiry. It is integral to the whole idea of knowledge-inquiry that, once knowledge has been acquired, it should be applied to help solve social problems. That social science at present includes discussion of social problems and how they are to be solved does not, in itself, go against the idea that knowledge-inquiry still prevails in this domain.[1]

I proceed as follows. First, I discuss in a bit more detail the global problem of climate change, and what we need to do about it — the most serious of the five global problems indicated in chapter three. I consider the question: What would a wise world be? Then I discuss how academia needs to be changed so that the activity of exploring problems of living and their possible solutions — including global problems — is put at the heart of the enterprise so that it becomes intellectually more fundamental than the pursuit of knowledge about social phenomena — intellectually more fundamental, indeed, than the pursuit of knowledge about natural phenomena. I consider then how we might go about feeding aim-oriented rationality into the fabric of the social world, into personal, institutional, and even global life. I conclude with a remark about the need to launch a campaign to bring about academic change so that wisdom-inquiry is put into practice in universities around the world.

The idea is first to try to *do* wisdom-inquiry by tackling a problem of living, in however sketchy, preliminary, and inadequate a fashion, and then draw general conclusions about how academia needs to be reorganized so as to accommodate and promote this vital wisdom-inquiry activity at the heart of the enterprise, so that universities may come to be rationally devoted to helping humanity make progress towards as good a world as possible.

Let us, then, look in a little more detail at climate change, and what we need to do about it.

Global Warming

Without doubt, our most serious global problem is that posed by climate change. It is already underway. Since the beginning of the industrial revolution, some 150 years ago, the amount of CO_2 in the atmosphere has risen by a third, and the amount of methane, a much more potent greenhouse gas, has doubled. The average global temperature has risen as a result by over 0.8 degrees centigrade, more than 80% of this increase having occurred since 1980. In recent years—I am writing in January 2013—glaciers have retreated, while on mountains, in the Himalayas, the Alps, and on the highest mountain in Africa, Kilimanjaro, and elsewhere ice and snow have progressively melted. Arctic ice, recently, has decreased dramatically every successive Summer, so much so that some climate scientists fear that in only a few years it will all melt away and there will be ice-free ocean at the North Pole in the summer. Freak weather events—hurricanes, torrential rains, flooding, drought, heat waves, and forest fires—have increased in intensity and frequency, just as predicted by computer modelling of the impact of global warming. In the UK, 2012 was very nearly the wettest year on record, just beaten by 2000. And as I write, multiple forest fires are reported to be blazing destructively all over Australia, after a period of drought and record temperatures.

As to how and why more CO_2 in the atmosphere causes a rise in average global temperature, this is very well established and understood. When the earth's surface receives light from the sun, it emits invisible infrared radiation which is absorbed and re-emitted by CO_2 in the atmosphere, some of this re-emitted radiation returning to the earth's surface. In this way, CO_2 traps heat from the sun, and the more CO_2 there is, so the more heat is trapped, and up goes the temperature. That CO_2

has this effect was established empirically by John Tyndall long ago in 1859.[2]

In order to keep the average global temperature rise below one degree centigrade we would have to keep the amount of CO_2 in the atmosphere below 350 parts per million (ppm). But it is already 380 ppm, due to human intervention. Why has this not already produced a one degree rise, or more? Because, as I remarked in chapter three, there is a delay in the global climate system. It takes 30 years or more for increased CO_2 in the atmosphere to produce its full effects of temperature rise. We have already put more than enough CO_2 in the atmosphere to cause a one degree or more rise in global temperature during the next thirty years or so.

A mere rise of one degree centigrade in the average global temperature will have devastating consequences.[3] The Midwest of the USA, because of drought, will be converted from being the rich agricultural land that it is at present into desert. It will be far worse than the Dust Bowl of the 1930s. Under the thin soils that at present support grass and corn there is sand, once the dunes of an ancient desert. The coming drought will kill vegetation, the thin topsoil will be blown away, and the sand dunes will come to prevail over what is now a vast region of high agricultural productivity. Elsewhere, in Australia, the Queensland tropical rain forests will be drastically reduced in size. Hundreds of species of plants and animals, some going back to the time of the dinosaurs, will become extinct. The Great Barrier Reef, and other coral reefs all over the world — the tropical rain forests of the oceans in that they sustain a multitude of fish species — will die, becoming bleached and barren, as a result of oceans becoming more acidic due to the absorption of CO_2.[4] Pacific islands will disappear as sea levels rise due to melting ice:[5] Tuvalu (9,000 inhabitants); Kiribati (78,000); the Marshall Islands (58,000); and the Maldives in the Indian Ocean (with 269,000 inhabitants). Those living on low-lying coastal regions round the world will also be under threat as sea levels rise and storms intensify.

If we manage to keep CO_2 in the atmosphere to 400 ppm we might be able to keep the temperature rise to two degrees centigrade. But a two-degree rise brings further disasters. Europe in the summer of 2003 experienced an unprecedented heat wave. Around 35,000 people in Europe died prematurely as a result. Such death-dealing heat waves will occur, not once in a blue moon, but on average every other summer. Some areas, such as parts of India and China, will experience heavier monsoons and much more flooding, while other areas, such as northern China, will be bereft of monsoons, desert conditions coming to prevail as a result. Dry regions, such as Peru and California, which depend on melting ice on mountains for summer water, will be deprived of this vital flow of water because the mountain ice will have disappeared permanently. Sea levels will continue to rise as Greenland ice melts.[6] CO_2 absorbed by the oceans turns the oceans acidic, as we have seen. This prevents plankton from forming their calcium carbonic structure (and even dissolves this structure), so that, as a result, Plankton begin to die out. Plankton are at the base of the food chain in the oceans. As plankton die, so too do all ocean fish, seals, and whales. The oceans become empty of life. And life on land suffers too. With a rise of two degrees, it has been estimated, a third of all species on earth become extinct.[7]

In order to keep the temperature rise no higher than two degrees, we would need to make immediate rapid and drastic reductions in CO_2 emissions, which seems unlikely. If CO_2 emissions world-wide continue to rise at something like their present rate to produce a CO_2 level of 450 ppm, the temperature will rise by three degrees.

A three-degree rise causes Botswana and surrounding areas in Africa, already parched today, to become bereft of rain and incapable of supporting agriculture and people. Across the Atlantic, the vast tracts of the Amazonian rain forests, rich with an incredible diversity of life, will turn to desert, with the release of billions of tonnes of carbon into the atmosphere.[8] There are recent signs that this is already underway. Early in 2013, NASA announced that an area of the rain forest twice the size of California is suffering from drought.[9] Tropical rain forests in Indonesia and Malaysia are likewise threatened. Snow and ice all but disappear from the Himalayas, which means that the Indus river, which depends on melting snow and ice, will dry up in summer with devastating consequences for agriculture and habitability for Pakistan. The Colorado River in the USA and Mexico endures a similar fate. Vast quantities of Greenland and Antarctic ice melt and cause ocean levels to rise. Manhattan suffers from repeated flooding as a result of rising sea levels and increasingly intense storms, and may have to be abandoned. Other coastal cities and areas around the world will be similarly threatened, including London and those parts of the Netherlands below sea level today. Land north of the Mediterranean, in Spain, France, Italy, and Greece, much of which today is so productive agriculturally, becomes desert. As Mark Lynas puts it, "The Sahara will have jumped the Strait of Gibraltar and begun marching north".[10]

If CO_2 rises as high as 550 ppm, which it will do if we fail to curtail emissions until 2050, the temperature will rise four degrees. Immense quantities of ice in Greenland and Antarctica continue to melt, raising sea levels even further. Vast tracts of land around the globe, at present densely populated and agriculturally productive, have to be abandoned because of flooding, drought, desert conditions. World food production collapses. Millions of people, possibly billions, die as a result of hunger, heat, flooding, and drought. There is every chance of war, as millions of people seek to migrate from land that no longer supports life, and are resisted by those struggling to live in adjacent, much compromised regions.

650 parts per million CO_2 in the atmosphere and the temperature will rise by five degrees, while if CO_2 goes up to 800 ppm, the temperature would rise by six degrees. There would be a different planet. Sea levels might eventually rise by 65 metres, drowning much of Britain and reshaping the continents. Extinction of species might be so massive that it could compare with the mass extinction that occurred at the end of the Permian period, 251 million years ago, when, it is estimated, 95% of all

species disappeared and life on earth nearly died.[11] Humanity would be reduced to a few million people eking out an existence in parts of Canada, Greenland, Scandinavia, northern Russia, and parts of Antarctica as the ice melts. We would survive, but our world would be devastated.

How do we know all this? How confident can we be that these predictions are correct? We cannot be absolutely confident that what I have outlined is correct in every detail. Perhaps a mere rise of one degree centigrade will not be sufficient to turn the Midwest of the USA into a dust bowl—but, at the time of writing, drought is already a problem in Nebraska and neighbouring States. Perhaps more than a rise of three degrees centigrade is required to destroy the Amazon rain forests—but recently NASA reported that an area of forest twice the size of California is suffering severely from drought.[12] The account I have given is based on the predictions of many different computer models of the climate. Though constructed in different ways, these models are broadly in agreement in what they predict. These models have successfully predicted recent climate changes, and more dramatic climate changes that have occurred in the past.

In so far as climate scientists have erred, it has been on the side of caution. The ice of glaciers, mountains and, above all, the arctic has melted much more rapidly than expected a decade or so ago. Sea levels have risen more rapidly, and temperatures have risen more rapidly, especially in the Poles, than expected. A decade ago, climate scientists thought it would be possible to keep the temperature rise below two degrees centigrade. Now it is feared it will rise by three degrees, or even higher.

The most alarming aspect of our situation is the existence of a number of positive feedback effects which come into play as the temperature rises—some of which have already come into play—and which threaten to cause the temperature to spiral up out of control. Arctic ice melts, and as a result less sunlight is reflected back into space, because ocean water is not such a good mirror as ice, and so the planet heats up even more. The Russian Steppes thaw and release vast quantities of methane, twenty times more powerful a greenhouse gas than CO_2. The oceans warm up, and absorb less CO_2 as a result, which means more lingers in the atmosphere to contribute more to rising temperatures. Plants subject to drought absorb much less CO_2 which means, again, more lingers in the atmosphere to add to global warming. And if tropical rain forests, in Brazil, Indonesia, Australia, and elsewhere, succumb to drought and become deserts, catastrophic quantities of CO_2 will be released into the atmosphere. Perhaps the most alarming positive feedback mechanism arises from the lurking presence of vast quantities of methane hydrate beneath the ocean in the arctic and elsewhere. Methane hydrate is a combination of methane and water kept in an ice-like condition by the intense cold and pressure found at the bottom of oceans. But as the temperature of the ocean rises, methane hydrate may melt and cause vast quantities of methane to erupt into the atmosphere, adding further to global warming.

Possibly even more alarming still, we now know that the climate has fluctuated many time in the past, sometimes changes coming about very rapidly indeed, in a matter of decades,[13] periods warmer than today by five or six degrees centigrade or more being associated with greater amounts of CO_2 in the atmosphere, there being evidence for some of these fluctuations that increased levels of CO_2 came first, and thus are almost certain to be the cause of the higher temperatures.[14]

The threats posed by climate change are all too clear. Unless we take action millions, possibly billions, will die as a result. As a matter of urgency, we need to bring down global CO_2 emissions to safe levels.[15] International treaties and agreements have been reached—the United Nations Framework Convention on Climate Change of 1992 and the Kyoto Protocol of 1997. These have led to international conferences on successive years at Buenos Aires, Bonn, The Hague, Marrakesh, New Delhi, Milan, Buenos Aires, Montreal, Nairobi, Bali, Poznań, Copenhagen, Cancún, Durban, and Doha in Qatar in 2012. Governments in Europe and elsewhere have backed the development of sustainable sources of energy—primarily solar and wind—and have supported energy efficiency in homes and elsewhere. Firms have been created to develop sustainable energy: wind, solar, wave, tidal, geothermal, biomass. Nicholas Stern produced his much discussed Review in 2006 in which he argued that there is a strong economic case for taking action now to prevent global warming as opposed to leaving matters until later.[16] The transition town movement has helped communities to take steps locally to mitigate global warming.[17] Efforts have been made to slow down the destruction of tropical rain forests, in Brazil, Indonesia, and elsewhere. But, despite all these treatises and efforts, global emissions of CO_2 continue to increase. Indeed, the rate of increase is increasing.[18] We are heading towards disaster.

A part of the problem has been the failure of the USA to ratify the Kyoto Protocol, objecting to the non-inclusion of developing nations. This ignores that the problem has been created by industrially advanced, wealthy nations — and above all by the USA which, until recently, emitted more CO_2 than any other nation. Other factors that have stymied the kind of decisive international action that is required include: rather effective propaganda and misinformation of climate change deniers;[19] the tendency of some parts of the media, such as the BBC, to give equal time and weight to what climate scientists and climate deniers have to say in the interest of "balance"; a mood of fatalism and helplessness among many who appreciate global warming poses a real threat; and the economic recession of recent years which has drawn attention away from the climate change crisis we face.

But by far the most important factor delaying action has been the lack of wisdom-inquiry universities shouting from the rooftops about the potential menace of climate change, and the urgent need to take decisive action.

We have, it seems, only a few years to act if we are to avoid dangerous increases in temperature. The longer we wait, the worse it will be.[20] As a matter of supreme urgency we need to wind down our use of coal, oil, and gas for power, transport, and heating, and develop instead as rapidly as possible sustainable sources of energy: solar, wind, wave, tidal, hydroelectric, and nuclear. This demands government intervention, support, and funding. We need to put the planet on a war footing, this time fighting a common enemy. International agreements are essential. Combustion of oil, petrol, gas, and coal needs to be taxed at a steadily increasing rate, clearly announced, so that alternative methods of power production and transport become increasingly viable economically.[21] It may be that carbon rationing needs to be introduced, to ensure carbon emissions are reduced in both effective and equable ways.[22] Developed nations need to take a lead in the matter: they have caused most of the problem so far. Developing nations need massive help from developed nations to enable their economies to grow in ways which avoid carbon pollution. Solar power stations need to be built in deserts, such as the Sahara, as rapidly as possible. Nuclear power stations need to be built and brought online. (The disaster at Fukushima in March 2011 has unfortunately stiffened resistance to nuclear power.) In particular, Integral Fast Reactors need to be developed and built: these have the potential to run on nuclear waste produced by current nuclear power plants. Thorium power stations should be developed. Thorium is plentiful and, unlike uranium-235, cannot be used to make nuclear bombs.

Our homes, offices, factories, and streets need to become more energy-efficient. Public transport needs government subsidies to make it as inexpensive as possible. Electric vehicles need development (but this only helps if electric power is itself produced in a way that does not cause carbon pollution). We may have to become largely vegetarian: it has been calculated that the processes that bring meat to the table contribute 18% of all CO_2 emissions in the world, more than transport.[23]

Little of this is likely to happen without public understanding and consent. It is here that the wisdom-inquiry university has such a vital role to play. It has, as a basic task, to promote public understanding of what our problems of living are, and what we need to do about them.

Two final points concerning climate change. First, this global problem interacts with the four other global problems, briefly discussed in chapter three, in a number of different, complex ways. Population growth exacerbates global warming. Global warming may well lead to war, if populated regions of the earth become uninhabitable and people attempt to migrate. War could distract attention away from dealing with the threats of climate change. It will be the poor of the world who will suffer most from the consequences of global warming—just those who are least responsible for bringing it about. Global warming threatens natural habitats, and threatens to bring about mass extinction of species. If tropical rain forests turn to deserts as a result of drought, not only will this cause devastating loss of species, it will further exacerbate global warming.

Second, in order to tackle problems of climate change—and our other global problems—we need to call upon, and inter-relate, a wide range of specialities and domains of public life: climate science, engineering, nuclear physics, economics, government, public policy, public attitudes, education, experts on solar, wind, tidal, hydro, and geothermal power—to name a few. The social, educational, political, economic, and scientific and technological are inextricably intermingled. This obvious point will prove to be important when we come to consider how the wisdom-inquiry university should be shaped so as best to help humanity tackle global problems effectively, intelligently, and humanely.

What Is a Wise World?

Before we consider how universities need to be organized and pursued so as to help humanity make progress towards a wise world we need some kind of answer to the key question, long deferred: What is a wise world? What we take our problems of living to be, especially of course our social, political, and global problems, will depend, to some extent at least, on what we take to be the ideal world society we should aim to achieve in the long term.

It might seem rather foolishly idealistic to consider what would be a wise world, confronted as we are by likely future disasters of rising temperatures, floods and drought, food scarcity, hunger, starvation, mass migration, and possibly war. Actually, it is all the other way round. Just because we are faced by these likely future calamities, it has become a matter of extreme urgency that we create a wiser world — so that we have the wisdom to reduce CO_2 emissions as rapidly as possible, and deal in as humane and effective a way as possible with the disasters rising temperatures are likely to result in.

The answer of this book is easy to state. A wise world is one that is able to make progress towards, or sustain, as good a world as possible. It is a world that puts wisdom-inquiry into practice in its institutions of learning and research, and puts aim-oriented rationality into practice in its worthwhile, problematic personal, institutional, social, and global endeavours so that people may realize what is genuinely of value to them in life. Roughly, a wise world is a means towards a good world. In creating a wise world we create the capacity, the active desire, the policies and actions, to create a good world.

At once the question becomes: What is a good world? What kind of ideal social world ought we to seek to achieve in the long term?

The task here is not to define what "good world" *means*. It is rather to specify what our *aim* should be in the long term in seeking to make progress towards as good a world as possible. The task is to specify a global state of affairs which is both *realizable* and genuinely *desirable* — the most valuable world society that can be achieved in the long term.

In chapter two I stressed, when discussing aim-oriented rationality, that the aim of achieving a good or genuinely civilized[24] world is inherently and profoundly problematic — problematic not just because of the difficulties of achieving it, but even more, perhaps, because of problems inherent in the aim itself. It is problematic because people have very different ideas as to what does constitute civilization. People's interests, values, and ideals clash. Most views about what constitutes Utopia, an ideally civilized society, have been *both* unrealizable *and* profoundly undesirable, and 20th-century efforts to create an ideal society, whether of the left or right politically, all too often led to disastrous outcomes.

For all sorts of reasons, we do not know what it is possible to achieve: what the planet can sustain,[25] what may become poss- ible as a result of new technology and methods of agriculture, what our inherent human nature can adapt to and sustain, what social arrangements are feasible and sustainable. Might we one day, no doubt far into the future, be able to dispense with armies, and even with the police, or will we always need them? Will there not always be some criminals, or the criminally insane? Will we not always need to guard against clever social psychopaths seizing power, even in democracies?

Even our best ideas as to what would constitute a good, civilized world seem fraught with paradox and contradiction. A basic aim of legislation for civilization, we may well hold, ought to be to increase freedom by restricting it: this again brings out the inherently problematic character of the aim. Wealth enhances freedom. If freedom is for everyone, and not just for some, then wealth too should be for everyone, and not just for some. In a civilized world the degree of equality would be established (by taxation and other means) that is compatible with, and facilitates, the greatest degree of freedom for all: such a balancing of equality and freedom is, however, clearly, inher- ently problematic and controversial.

There is another reason for holding that what constitutes a wise world is problematic: we cannot experience the diverse candidate social worlds that we would need to experience in order to come to an informed judgment as to which is best. And even if we could, how would we be able to judge properly their relative, no doubt complex, merits and demerits? We can attempt to compensate for the extreme limitations of our experi- ence by vividly and accurately imagining realistic possibilities, and comparing the desirability of different societies at various times and places, but such attempts are bound to be limited in what they can achieve.

A good world would be so organized that people can realize what is of value to them in life, individually and together, in so far as that is possible. People would share equally in sustaining, creating, and enjoying what is of value, in so far as this is possible. But what is of value? Is anything ultimately of value, given that we all, at best, grow old and die, and everything we seek to achieve in the end comes to nothing? And if what is of value is in the eye of the beholder, does not that mean that, objectively, nothing is of intrinsic value? Is there not, at best, merely the subjective illusion of value?

The inherently problematic character of the aim of achieving civilization means that we must employ aim-oriented rationality both in characterizing the aim, and in attempting to realize it.[26] In Figure 3 on page 36 I indicated how the aim of achieving a good, civilized world can be characterized hierarchically, from a highly unspecific and unproblematic characterization at the top (level 7) to a much more specific and problematic characterization lower down (at level 3). It is vital not just to *characterize* civilization in this hierarchical fashion but, above all, to construe our aim in this way, and put aim-oriented rationality into practice, in our efforts to make progress towards a good, civilized world. To summarize what I argued for in chapter two, the hierarchical structure of aims and methods of aim-oriented rationality helps us improve our problematic aims, and associated methods, as we act, as we live, by means of imaginative and critical exploration of possibilities, and by means of experience, what we enjoy and suffer as a result of seeking to achieve this or that aim, implement this or that policy. Aim-oriented rationality facilitates resolution of disagreement and conflict in that it helps us distinguish what we agree about (high up in the hierarchy) and what we disagree about (low down in the hierarchy), and then helps us live with or resolve what we disagree about. It provides the means to assess the relative merits of rival political philosophies and philosophies of life, in terms of agreed assumptions (high up in the hierarchy) and what we experience when we seek to put these philosophies into practice, in somewhat the same way as rival theories can be assessed in science. As a result of importing into life progress-achieving methods generalized from science, we may hope to get into life something of the progressive success achieved by science. There is the hope that, echoing what goes on in science, as we make progress towards as good a world as possible, we improve our (more or less specific) aims and methods — our ideas about how to achieve progress — there being something like positive feedback between an improving social world and improving ideas about how to make social progress. We learn how to learn.[27]

Some views about what features a good world should possess will be relatively uncontroversial (although what precise form these features should take and how they should be reconciled with one another are likely to be more controversial). These features include democracy, liberty, sustainability, peace, justice, prosperity, a free market organized and regulated so that it benefits everyone and not just a wealthy few, education and health care for all. In a good world, our five global problems will have been solved. I now discuss briefly four features of a good world as I see it, that are likely to be more controversial.

First, a good world would be a very much more equal world than what we have today. Something like a billion people live in abject poverty, in Asia, central Africa, and South America, without safe water, sufficient food, adequate shelter, health care, employment, or education, while most of those of us who live in industrially advanced countries have all of the above, and very much more. A good world would not tolerate such glaring differences in wealth, and would work hard to eliminate such global poverty if it had inherited it from the past.

There are also dramatic differences in wealth in some wealthy countries — most notably the UK, Portugal, and, even more so, the USA.[28] Half of the assets of the USA are owned by just 400 people.[29] Michael Meacher MP highlighted recently just how grotesque inequality has become in the UK by pointing out that *The Sunday Times* rich list published in 2012 reveals that "the 1,000 richest persons in the UK have increased their wealth by so much in the last 3 years — £155bn — that they themselves alone could pay off the entire UK budget deficit and still leave themselves with £30bn to spare", which, Meacher adds, "should be enough to keep the wolf from the door".[30] And this during a period of recession and severe benefit cuts that have caused the poor to become considerably poorer. In their devastating book *The Spirit Level*, Richard Wilkinson and Kate Pickett have produced a mass of evidence to show that, among wealthy nations, everyone benefits from equality. In more equal nations, such as Japan and Scandinavian countries, people are healthier, live longer, are less obese, suffer less from mental health problems, do better educationally, and are less likely to commit murder, go to prison, or suffer from drug abuse than people living in nations where there is greater inequality, such as the UK and the USA. Even the wealthy benefit. Among the wealthy, people die younger in the USA than they do in Japan.[31] I find the argument for greater equality convincing, and the counter-arguments that equality undermines both liberty and wealth for all unconvincing and little better than special pleading on behalf of the very wealthy.

Second, in a good world, in my view, businesses and other ventures and institutions would be run on cooperative lines as far as possible; ownership, decision-making, responsibility, and profits (where relevant) being shared. The cooperative movement in Mondragon in the Basque region of Spain provides us with a demonstration of what is possible. It began in 1956 in the time of Franco's dictatorship, when a group of peasants consulted their local priest, Jose Maria Arizmendi, about starting up a cooperative. Since then, the movement has gone from strength to strength. In the 1980s, the various companies joined together as the Mondragon Cooperative Corporation—now the Basque Country's largest corporation, and the seventh largest in Spain, the largest worker cooperative in the world. Cooperative members own and direct each company. They hire and fire managing directors, the reverse of what occurs in the rest of the business world. The highest paid workers earn no more than 6.5 times as much as the lowest paid, in contrast to US corporations where top directors can expect to earn 400 times as much as the average worker.[32]

A wise, good world would seek, as far as possible, to resolve conflicts and problems of living in cooperatively rational ways. As I mentioned in chapter two, there is a spectrum of ways in which conflicts are resolved, from murder or war at one end to the cooperatively rational discovery and implementation of the most desirable, just resolution at the other end. A wise world would seek to move conflict resolution away from the violent end of the spectrum towards the cooperatively rational end.

Cooperative rationality is required in order to enhance individual liberty. Inevitably, on a crowded planet, interests and actions will clash. Cooperative rationality may well be required to resolve such clashes in ways which do the best justice to the interests of all those involved.[33] Even in a good world, however, cooperative action would need to be qualified or restricted in various circumstances. A cooperative endeavour that involves everyone in all decision-making all the time is likely to be hopelessly inefficient. Some delegation of decision-making is likely to be necessary—as Mondragon recognizes.[34]

Third, a good world would, in my view, possess a democratic world government. In our intricately interconnected modern world, all the overwhelming reasons for having a democratic government for a *nation* apply with equal force to the whole world. The UN is no substitute. Democratic world government would not, of course, in itself solve all our problems. Democracies can sustain corruption, gross inequality, crime, armed conflict. But even if not sufficient, democratic world government would seem to be necessary for a good world. It is of course true that horrendous problems of prejudice and organization lie in the way of creating such a government.

Fourth, in requiring a good world to be sustainable, we should interpret that to include the preservation of as much of the miraculous diversity of living things we have on earth today as possible. A good world preserves tropical rain forests and other natural habitats—and seeks to maintain the multiplicity of species in existence today.

At this point it may be objected that the whole approach being presupposed here is misconceived. Efforts to make progress towards as good a world as possible should concentrate on getting rid of the worst manifest, specific, current ills that we can do something about: hunger, poverty, curable and preventable disease, corruption, lack of health care, dictatorships, people subject to armed conflict. This approach does not need to reach improbable agreement about what our long term goal of achieving an ideally civilized world should be. It does not strive to attain such a distant, problematic goal. Rather, it concerns itself with unnecessary human suffering and death in the world now, immediately recognizable and undeniable — suffering and death which we can do something about.

This is, surely, absolutely the right approach. We do need to concentrate on saving people now from unnecessary suffering, wasted lives, and death. But we also need to keep alive imaginative and critical thinking about what our long term aims should be, and what the long term consequences of our current actions are likely to be. In acting to relieve suffering now, we may need to be aware of what is desirable in the long term because this may influence what form our current actions should take. And some actions that we undeniably need to take now may not be to relieve current human suffering at all. This is true by and large of actions to stop habitat destruction and the extinction of species. And it is true of actions to stop global warming: here, primarily, what is at issue is the suffering of future generations, perhaps for centuries or even millennia to come — although as the dire consequences of global warming — such as droughts, floods, and food shortages — become increasingly apparent, immediate suffering becomes more of an issue.

There is another objection I must now briefly confront. In committing academia to helping humanity make progress towards as good a world as possible, we thereby commit academia to a *political* programme. But how can this possibly be acceptable or justifiable? The proper task of academia is to improve knowledge, technological know-how, and understanding, thereby providing us with means to help us achieve ends in life we decide for ourselves, personally, democratically, or in other ways. It cannot conceivably be acceptable for unelected academics to decide for the rest of us what our goals in life should be, what kind of world we should strive to achieve.

This conclusion is correct. It cannot be right for academics to determine for the rest of us what our goals in life should be. In chapter two I stated emphatically that wisdom-inquiry academia needs just sufficient power to maintain its independence, but no more. Wisdom-inquiry academia does not decide for the rest of us what we should think, what our values, ideals, or life aims should be, how we should live. It is as anxious to learn from as to teach the public. It adopts its values, objectives, and political ends *rationally*—that is, as a result of open, imaginative, and critical exploration of possibilities and an appeal to evidence, argument, and counter-argument. And it pursues its ideals and political objectives by means of reason and public education, not manipulation, persuasion, or coercion. A basic political objective is to help all of us—or as many as possible— educate ourselves as to what our problems are, what we need to do about them, so that we may be in a better position to achieve what is genuinely of value to us in life, individually, and together as a group, an institution, a nation, humanity in its entirety.

It is tempting to think that, whereas knowledge-inquiry is wholly objective, factual, free of value assumptions and politics, wisdom-inquiry by contrast is burdened with value and political assumptions and commitments, however rationally adopted and pursued, the objectivity of inquiry thereby being undermined or even subverted. But this is a false contrast, as we saw in chapter two. Knowledge-inquiry makes value and political assumptions too, in its priorities of research, in what it deems to be of value to develop knowledge about, and in deciding to whom, to what bodies, new knowledge is to be delivered, and for what purposes. The big difference between the two kinds of inquiry is not, then, that one is free of values and politics while the other is not. It is, rather, that the value and political assumptions of knowledge-inquiry are denied, repressed, and are therefore irrational, and likely to be all the more dogmatically upheld as a result. Knowledge-inquiry, unable to criticize or challenge the value and political assumptions of the society in which it is set (because of the official idea it seeks objective knowledge of truth) is all the more likely to reflect merely the value and political assumptions of the status quo — the social milieu in which it exists. Wisdom-inquiry by contrast subjects value and political assumptions and goals to sustained, explicit imaginative and critical exploration. These assumptions and goals are rationally upheld and pursued, and it is an important part of the task of wisdom-inquiry to question, to criticize and challenge the values and politics of the status quo. In making assumptions concerning values and politics explicit and open to critical appraisal, wisdom-inquiry has greater rigour, rationality, and objectivity than knowledge-inquiry.

It is vital that wisdom-inquiry puts aim-oriented rationality into practice. If it did not, there would inevitably, at some point, be something arbitrary about the value and political assumptions of academia. Aim-oriented rationality transforms the realm of values, ideals, aims, and political objectives and programmes so that it ceases to be merely arbitrary and becomes that about which we can learn. The hierarchical framework of assumptions and goals of aim-oriented rationality is designed specifically to facilitate learning as to what is of value, what goals we should pursue, what political programmes we should seek to enact. And learning goes in both directions, non-academics having as much, or more, to teach academics as the other way round. It is, of course, a cooperative endeavour.

One final question remains to be considered in this section: What, ultimately, is of value? This is a question I have discussed at length elsewhere.[35] Here I will be brief. Relativist or subjectivist views about value are widely held: there is merely the subjective illusion of value of this group, or this person, nothing being of value objectively, in reality. Reasons for holding such subjectivist views tend, however, to be invalid. I shall consider four.

The first is a moral argument. An objectivist or realist about value would dogmatically *know* what is of value and would, like the Victorians, impose his values on others, if necessary with force. In order to avoid such morally obnoxious attitudes and actions we must adopt a subjectivist view, and hold that it is up to individuals to decide for themselves what is of value, nothing objectively, in reality, being of value. But what is wrong with dogmatic realism is not the realism—as the subjectivist thinks—but the dogmatism. Subjectivism actually *intensifies* dogmatism. The dogmatic realist knows he is right, although it makes sense to say he is wrong, but it does not even make sense to say that the subjectivist is wrong. We need to distinguish three positions: (1) dogmatic realism, (2) subjectivism, and (3) conjectural realism. (3) holds that value-features of people, actions, institutions, artefacts, and aspects of the natural world are real, objectively existing features and, precisely for that reason, we may be wrong in our views about what is of value: these views need to be held as conjectures. (3) allows us to hold that aspects of life and existence are in reality of value, we may be more or less wrong in what we hold to be of value, but we can *learn* about what is of value. (2) permits none of this. In opposing (1), we need to adopt (3), not (2).

The second argument has to do with perception. In order to discover for ourselves what is of value, and not just parrot the judgments of others, we need to attend to our feelings and desires. But that makes what is of value irredeemably subjective. But no, it does not. We may compare perception of value to perception of colour. We can only see what is red if we have the visual experience of redness, but that does not mean redness is subjective.[36] Likewise, we can only see what is good if we desire and feel, but that does not mean what is good is a purely subjective matter. Just as there can be perceptual illusions and hallucinations, so too with what is of value: not everything that feels good is good, and not everything we desire is desirable, as I have already remarked.

The third argument is epistemological in character. People disagree dramatically about what is of value in life, and hence it cannot make sense to hold that what is of value is something objective, an aspect of reality. But this argument is clearly invalid. People disagree dramatically about undeniably factual matters, even in science, where an objective reality indisputably exists. And we need to recognize that, as I put it many years ago, "That which is of value in existence, associated with human life, is inconceivably, unimaginably, richly diverse in character".[37] That people find different things of value arises often from the fact that they prize different aspects of all that is of value, and need not constitute disagreement at all.

The fourth argument is metaphysical. Value realism must be the view that there is some mysterious stuff—value, or quality as Robert Pirsig once called it[38]—which pervades the universe and might perhaps, one day, be captured in a test tube as a newly discovered fluid. This is nonsense. But it is entirely the wrong way to think of value-features in the world. Typical familiar value-features of people are: friendly, mean, jolly, stern, witty, courageous, warm-hearted, dull, frivolous, shifty, kind, spontaneous, strong-willed, earnest, gloomy, calculating, mischievous, cold, boring, gushing, loyal, ambitious, argumentative, generous. These are both descriptive and value-laden, factual and imbued with value. People, like works of art in a somewhat different way, are essentially value-imbued, morality-imbued beings: we cannot describe a personality, we cannot state facts about a personality, without employing value-imbued factual terms of the kind just indicated, any more than we can describe a work of art as a work of art without employing analogous aesthetic terms, value-imbued factual terms. Value-features are familiar to us all, and do not require some dubious metaphysical entity to exist.

And what is supremely of value in existence? My conjecture is that it is mutual love between persons and, more generally, life lived lovingly, so that one enjoys and cares for that which deserves to be loved, actually and potentially.[39]

The Wisdom-Inquiry University:
Problem-Solving Rationality

How ought social inquiry, the humanities, and other relevant disciplines to be organized and conducted within the context of wisdom-inquiry, so as to devote reason to helping humanity

create a wiser world? What is to be learnt from our all-too-brief
discussion, above and in chapter 3, of the five global problems:
climate change, war, population growth, world poverty, and
destruction of natural habitats and extinction of species? I
answer these questions in two stages, employing first problem-
solving rationality, and then aim-oriented rationality.

As I envisage wisdom-inquiry, it would seek to represent
the current state of inquiry in the form of an intricate pyramid
structure of problems and attempted solutions, our fundamental problem at the apex, problems becoming progressively
increasingly specialized and local in character as one goes down
the pyramid. This pyramid structure of problems and their
attempted solutions could readily be represented on a website,
available to all, the home page depicting the fundamental problems, other pages representing diverse more specialized problems, there being copious links to other websites dealing with
specialized problems in much greater detail and depth.

Our fundamental problem of both thought and life, embracing all other more specialized, more particular, and more personal problems, can be put like this:

(1) How can our human world, imbued with sensory qualities, consciousness, free will, meaning, and value, exist and
best flourish embedded as it is in the physical universe?

This is at the apex of the pyramid.[40] Or, perhaps not quite at the
apex, for we could formulate it in an even more general way as:

(0) How can the worlds of sentient life exist and best flourish
embedded as they are in the universe as it is?

(0) is more general than (1) in that it is not restricted to our
human world, to the world of human consciousness, and it does
not assume that the universe is more or less as modern physics
tells us it is.

Problem (1) is to be understood as straddling natural
science, social science and the humanities, technological science,
and our practical problems of living from the global to the per-

sonal. All our other problems, whether scientific, intellectual, technical, or practical, are aspects of, various special versions of, problem (1).

Problem (1) immediately divides into three (in each case the phrase "imbued with sensory qualities, consciousness, free will, meaning, and value" is understood to be included):

(2a) The fundamental philosophical problem: How is it *possible* for our human world to exist embedded in the physical universe?

(2b) The fundamental problem of knowledge and understanding: How is our human world in fact embedded in the physical universe, and how and why did it come to exist?

(2c) The fundamental problem of living: How can our human world best flourish embedded as it is in the real world? What do we need to do to solve our problems of living, enable us to realize what is of value to us in life?

A few words, now, about these three problems in turn.

(2a) arises in an especially severe form because aim-oriented empiricism (expounded in chapter two) tells us that physics has already established that the universe is physically comprehensible (in so far as physics can establish anything theoretical at all). Physicalism — the thesis that the universe is physically comprehensible — though metaphysical, is nevertheless an established item of scientific knowledge. But if there is some as-yet undiscovered unified pattern of physical law running through all phenomena, which determines (perhaps probabilistically) how all events unfold in space and time, how is it possible for us to have free will? Are we not reduced to mere slaves of the physical universe, obliged to do what it dictates whatever illusion we may have that we are in charge? And if everything is, in the end, just physics, what becomes of the world as we experience it, imbued with colours, sounds, and tactile qualities, consciousness, meaning, and value? How can there be anything of value if everything is just physics? This "human world/physical universe" problem, as it may be called, has been a central preoccupation of philosophy ever since modern science began and brought to attention the first version of physicalism: the world is made up exclusively of corpuscles, minute physical particles, interacting by contact. Philosophy has, however, over the centuries, tackled the problem in a very seriously inadequate way. It has failed even to formulate the problem properly, let alone solve it. The first attempt at a solution was the one attributed to Descartes: the material world is as physics tells us it is, but in addition there is the world of conscious minds, associated in some mysterious way with living brains. Cartesian dualism scoops up sensory qualities, everything we experience, in the world around us and tucks it all into our minds, leaving behind in the material world nothing but mere, bleak physics. This view is of course confronted by severe problems. How is the mind related to the brain? If all we ever experience is our own mind, how can we ever know anything about the external world? After Descartes, philosophy became preoccupied by these problems — even when Cartesian dualism, which gave rise to them, had been rejected! In part as a result, philosophy after Descartes became increasingly dissociated from science. We need to remember that modern science began as an outgrowth of philosophy. Initially, it was called "natural" or "experimental" philosophy, and it brought together physics, chemistry, and other branches of natural science as we know it today, with diverse branches of philosophy: metaphysics, epistemology, methodology, philosophy of science — even theology. But then this integrated endeavour of natural philosophy to improve our knowledge and understanding of the universe and our place in it broke apart into natural science, and philosophy, and both of these two fragments suffered as a result, philosophy especially. Wisdom-inquiry would recreate natural philosophy, (2a) being taken as the fundamental problem of the more philosophical aspects of the integrated discipline.[41] Elsewhere, I have argued that we need to see physics as being concerned only with a highly select aspect of all that there is — that aspect which determines how events unfold. Physics, and all of science that is reducible to physics, does not and cannot say anything about the experiential realm. Thus the silence of physics about colours, sounds, all that we experience in the world around us, provides no grounds whatsoever for holding that these qualities do not really, objectively exist.[42]

Problem (2b) is to be interpreted in such a way that it embraces all of natural science, social science, and the humanities. Key theoretical ideas are the great explanatory theories of physics and cosmology, and Darwin's theory of evolution. The former help to pose the problem. If the universe really is more or less as modern physics tells us it is, then there is a profound mystery as to how human life—and life more generally—can exist, and can have come to be, with all its features and qualities of meaning and value. Darwinian theory is a key component of the solution: the miraculous diversity of life today has come about by means of the twin mechanisms of random inherited variation and natural selection: those variations best fitted to survive tend to be the ones that do survive. The fundamental task, however, is not just to explain the existence of life; it is, rather, to explain and understand the existence of life of meaning and value—the existence of all the richness of our human world: consciousness, free will, language, mutual understanding, love, friendship, laughter, joy, great art and science, and even perhaps such things as democracy and justice (in so far as these latter do exist). This requires that Darwinian theory is reinterpreted to do justice to the influence that *purposive action* and *learning* have on evolution.[43] Evolution by cultural means[44] becomes possible when animals can learn and imitate. A group of animals may change their way of life, not because of any genetic change, but purely as a result of learning and imitation. As a result of this change, what has survival value, and what does not, is changed too and, as a result, chance mutations which earlier would have had no survival value do now have survival value. The learnt change in way of life is a part of the cause of subsequent evolution. The giraffe only has a long neck because it was, prior to neck-lengthening mutations, striving to reach leaves to eat high up in trees. If it had not been so striving, the mutations would have had no survival value, and would have disappeared. Purposive action, in short, plays a vital role in Darwinian evolution, one which many evolutionary experts tend to ignore, or downplay.[45] A key point to appreciate is that the mechanisms of evolution themselves evolve as evolution proceeds, gradually incorporating purposive action in more and more important ways, so that elements of Lamarckism become integral to Darwinian evolution as learning and imitation come to play an increasingly influential role, and what one generation has learned (or "acquired") is passed onto subsequent generations, not genetically, but by means of imitation. We are unique among species in being the product of a massive amount of evolution by cultural means, first with the development of language, and then tools, technology, social traditions, culture, science, and art. Evolution by cultural means is, however, almost certainly long-standing and widespread among animals, very likely to be present whenever there is parental care, and thus in all probability going back to the dinosaurs.[46] Even plants can be construed as influencing evolution by means of purposive action—as long as we construe growth as a kind of purposive action.[47]

If evolution is understood in purely mechanistic, purposeless terms, an artificial and very un-Darwinian hiatus is created between our human world and the rest of life. This hiatus arises because we humans are essentially purposive beings, acting in the world in pursuit of our goals—and thus quite different from other animals if construed in purposeless terms. But if Darwinism is reinterpreted in the way I have indicated, this hiatus disappears. A Darwinian account of evolution melds seamlessly into archaeology, anthropology, and history. Our human world can be set naturally into the broader context of life on earth.

In order to tackle problem (2b), then, we need contributions that range from theoretical physics and cosmology, via biology and Darwinian theory, to anthropology, history, economics, sociology, psychology, and the study of international affairs. At the level that we are considering, high up in the pyramid, problems (2a) and (2b) and our best attempts at solutions need to be stated lucidly, accurately, and informally, so that ideas here are accessible to as many people as possible, whatever their educational background may be.

The failure to do this for the past century or so has been damaging intellectually, both within and without the university. Public learning about how our human world fits into Nature — so profoundly important for its own sake, and for the sake of understanding many of our problems of living and what we need to do about them — has been retarded as a result.

We come now to (2c), our fundamental problem of living. This presupposes, of course, that there is a solution to problem (2a), and we can in practice act so as to achieve what is of value to us in the real world, to some extent at least — something we all do and must in practice assume. (The paralysed, the ill, the mad, the imprisoned, the very poor, the mentally handicapped, the very young and old, may be, however, severely restricted in their capacity to act.)

One way to formulate (2c) would be to provide a vivid, realistic representation of a good world, and then depict ways in which our actual world fails to match up to this ideal. Or the worst cases of avoidable human suffering, impoverishment, and death could be depicted, together with accounts of what we need to do to reduce and eliminate this human deprivation.

Any such formulation of (2c) is bound to hide a multiplicity of complexities. Problems of living change dramatically as we move from person to person. A twelve-year-old boy living on the streets of Rio de Janeiro, a stockbroker working in the City in London, a woman begging on the streets of Mumbai, a party official in Beijing, a farmer working a smallholding in Poland, a Mafia boss in Moscow, an old man in his 70s dying of cancer: these people are confronted by very different problems of living. For each one of us, our problems of living change as time passes. Our problems have a complex hierarchical structure, from those problems that confront us from moment to moment, to those that may confront us for our entire life. Most of us solve most of our short term problems of living instinctively, without giving the matter a moment's thought, our brilliant brains doing all the work for us effortlessly. In addition to problems that confront individuals, there are problems that confront groups, institutions, enterprises of one kind or another, nations, the whole of humanity.

The pyramid representation of problems and attempted solutions of wisdom-inquiry needs to be developed further, of course, to take into account ever more numerous arrays of increasingly specialized problems and their attempted solutions as we descend towards the base of the pyramid. (2a) gives rise to the diverse branches of philosophy which would include: scientific metaphysics, epistemology, the mind–body problem, moral and political philosophy. (2b) gives rise to the diverse branches of natural and social science and the humanities, and to ever more specialized subordinate disciplines. And (2c) would give rise to global problems, regional and national problems, problems of particular aspects of life, institutions, and endeavours, and to problems confronted by individual persons in a variety of contexts. Communication in both directions needs to take place between fundamental and specialized problems and their attempted solutions, and between the different kinds of problem at all levels of specialization, from the philosophical and scientific to the practical.

It may seem that (2c) is quite different from (2a) and (2b) in that the latter require, for their solution, no more than the statement of their solution (plus arguments, observations, and other relevant factors to substantiate the claim that this is the solution), whereas the mere *statement* of the solution to (2c) — a set of proposals for action — leaves everything to be done. *Actions* solve (2c), not *words*. Knowledge-inquiry tends, however, to exaggerate this distinction. In seeking to solve (2a) and (2b) we endeavour to contribute to human knowledge and understanding. Whereas knowledge-inquiry downplays the significance of "human" here, wisdom-inquiry emphasizes it. Inquiry pursued to enhance knowledge and understanding for its own sake has, according to wisdom-inquiry, a profoundly social, educational, or *human* dimension to it: to enable non-academic *people*, the great world of humanity, to acquire a good understanding of what kind of world we live in, how we came to be, how we fit into the universe, what is of most value in life, and what kind of human world we might one day create. From a purely intellectual or cultural standpoint, all the theories, experiments, observations, and technicalities of science and scholarship are but means to facilitate the end of good public understanding of our world and our selves. Public education is a fundamental aspect, in short, of all three problems.

(2c) is nevertheless different from (2a) and (2b), in that, in addition to education, it concerns *action*, what we *do*, how we *live*.

It is important to note that in tackling problems of living, in exploring imaginatively and critically what our problems of living are and what we might do about them, we thereby contribute to our potential knowledge and understanding of ourselves, our human world. As I have argued in some detail elsewhere,[48] we need to distinguish two kinds of explanation and understanding, which may be called *scientific* and *personalistic*. We employ the first when we seek to predict—and thereby explain—phenomena by means of empirically confirmed theory. We employ the second when we seek to understand another person by imagining ourselves to be that other person, with that person's aims, desires, view of the world, relationships, plans, abilities, feelings, values, hopes, and fears.

Viewed from the perspective of knowledge-inquiry, scientific understanding seems vastly superior intellectually to personalistic understanding, in that the latter would seem to be subjective, personal, emotional, evaluative, intuitive, non-predictive, untestable, and thus non-rational and unscientific. And psychologists who study this kind of understanding as "theory of mind" tend to regard it as "folk psychology" which needs to be properly explained by scientific psychological theory.[49]

Viewed from the perspective of wisdom-inquiry, however, all this changes dramatically. According to wisdom-inquiry, articulating problems of living and proposing and critically assessing possible solutions, possible actions, are fundamental intellectual activities, more fundamental than tackling problems of knowledge. But this is just what we need to do in order to enhance personalistic understanding. I have a good personalistic understanding of another person if I know what his problems of living are and what he proposes to do about them. Thus, in stressing that tackling problems of living is intellectually fundamental, wisdom-inquiry thereby stresses that personalistic understanding is intellectually fundamental.

Scientific explanation of phenomena, whether natural or social, provides a basis for manipulation. As a result of being able to predict accurately and reliably what will occur in a variety of circumstances, we can create specific circumstances which will produce the outcome we desire. Thus explanatory theories in the natural sciences provide a basis for manipulating natural phenomena to become the artefacts of the modern age: cars, TV sets, medicine, aeroplanes, mobile phones. Somewhat less successfully, attempts are made to use explanatory theory in social science to manipulate people — in advertising for example.

Personalistic understanding does not make comparable reliable predictions, and is thus not such a good basis for manipulation. People are innovative and creative, not predictable automata, and can surprise us even if we do have a good personalistic understanding of them. Personalistic understanding is, however, absolutely essential for friendship, for love, and for cooperative action. In order to engage in some endeavour cooperatively, it is essential that participants can acquire personalistic understanding of each other as required, in order to understand each other's proposals, objectives, hopes, and difficulties. Personalistic understanding is thus also essential for science, since science is a cooperative endeavour.

In order to understand another personalistically, I need to know how that other person views his world. I may want to know this because I want to understand the person. On the other hand, I may want to improve my knowledge of the world, and the other person's view of the world may contribute to my own knowledge. Scientific knowledge arises in this way, the outcome of many scientists acquiring personalistic understanding of each other's views of phenomena, experimental results, research programmes, possible worlds, the *personal* dimensions in all this being suppressed, leaving the desired residue of ostensibly impersonal scientific knowledge. We need to see scientific and personalistic understanding dovetailing together, each dependent on the other.[50]

We need to engage in imaginative and critical exploration of problems of living even if our primary concern is not to help solve such problems, but rather to improve our understanding of our human world—our fellow human beings. Personalistic understanding is a vital ingredient of social inquiry and the humanities.

I come now to the key question of this chapter. How do universities need to be reorganized so as to give priority, in the appropriate way, to the task of helping humanity learn what our problems of living are, and what we need to do about them? What conclusions do we draw given the five global problems we have briefly considered: global warming, war, population growth, world poverty, destruction of natural habitats and extinction of species?

Wisdom-inquiry requires that the activity of tackling problems of living is at the heart of the university. It needs to be sustained and well-funded. Good ideas about what our problems are and what we need to do about them must be capable of influencing research and education in all other areas of academic inquiry: the physical and biological sciences, the technological sciences, the social sciences and humanities, medicine, and the professions such as law, architecture, planning, and teaching. All these fields likewise need to be capable of influencing thought about problems of living, when relevant. Above all, academics tackling problems of living need to pursue their work in such a way that their basic task is to help humanity learn what our problems are, and what we need to do about them. These academics need to engage with the public, with politicians, civil servants, journalists, broadcasters, lawyers, teachers, those in business and finance, campaigners, charities, and NGOs. Becoming a success in this field needs to be organized so that contributing to the enlightenment of humanity is what matters, not number of publications. Academic promotion and prizes need to be awarded accordingly.

Could all this be achieved by an internal transformation of social science and the humanities? The answer would seem to be: no. Those engaged in tackling problems of living must be drawn from a great variety of specialized disciplines, and not just from social science. In order to determine the character and gravity of some global problems—most obviously, global poverty and population growth—we do need to call upon social science. But in order to assess the seriousness of global warming, habitat destruction, and extinction of species we need climate scientists, geologists, biologists, agriculturalists, and experts on development. And in order to assess risks of armed conflict and war we need to call upon different specialists again: peace study experts, defence experts, students of current affairs, good journalists. Even more strikingly, when it comes to proposing and critically assessing possible solutions, possible and actual policies and actions, a whole army of specialists are required, drawn from a wide range of different disciplines: medicine, climate science, physics, chemistry, mechanical, electrical, and chemical engineering, biochemistry, molecular biology, ecology, futurology, environmental science, epidemiology, geography, architecture, information science, as well as economics, sociology, anthropology, social psychology—and a host of other specialities as well.[51] We live in a symbiotic relationship with technology. In tackling our problems of living we need to bring together both partners in this relationship, the social and the technological.

Would it suffice to do what my own university has done, University College London, and create a framework somewhat like the Grand Challenges Programme, mentioned in chapter four, which provides a context for specialists in different fields to work together on aspects of global problems on an ad hoc basis? Undeniably, this is a very important step in the right direction. But it does not, in my view, go far enough. There is not enough emphasis on imaginative creation and criticism of *policy*. Research groups come together for some specific research project and then, when the project is finished, return to their specialized fields of research. The Programme does not create the sustained research activity that is required, a *tradition* of problems of living research. Hardly anything has been done, so far, concerning education. And the whole Programme is restricted almost entirely to *research*, and does not engage with the public, the politicians, humanity at large, in the way that is required.

Can we leave it to the diverse specialists to do the work that is required? Again: no. Specialists will always be lured into doing more research and away from the vital and heartbreaking activity of attempting to communicate with the public. And besides, campaigning to get a hearing for some global problem may be difficult to reconcile with the frame of mind required to do specialized scientific research.

We need, I think, a whole new faculty in the university, alongside faculties devoted to physical science, biological science, engineering, social science and the humanities—the Faculty of Problems of Living Research. I imagine that this would consist of a number of departments, each devoted to some more or less specific global or regional problem—or perhaps to some characteristic kind of problem encountered by many individuals. There would be, perhaps, a department, more general and philosophical than the others, concerned with problems of living in general. There would be links with the shadow national and world governments mentioned in chapter two (points 22 and 23). Those working in this new faculty would be a new breed of academic, in that they would combine expertise in some specialist discipline with a broader knowledge concerning problems of living, a capacity to work with specialists from other disciplines, an ability to imagine future possibilities for humanity, and a flair for engaging with the public.

Despite what I have said above, the Faculty of Problems of Living Research might be created as an outgrowth of social science and the humanities as these exist in universities at present, appropriate specialists from engineering, climate science, biology, planning, and so on being incorporated as required. What matters of course is that the faculty acquires sufficient funding and status to be able to interact fruitfully with the rest of academia and take up its basic task to help humanity resolve conflicts and problems of living in ways that tend away from the violent end of the spectrum towards the cooperatively rational end.

I conclude this section with a remark about economics. Unlike other social sciences, economics has one fundamental problem of living at its basis that it quite clearly exists to help solve. Put crudely, it might be formulated as: How can wealth best be created and distributed? It follows at once that, in order to be organized and conducted rationally (rigorously), and in such a way as to be of maximum benefit to humanity, economics must give intellectual priority to the tasks of (1) articulating, and improving the articulation of, the fundamental problem to be solved, and (2) proposing and critically assessing possible solutions — possible *actions*, economic strategies, government policies, ideas about how to organize businesses, and so on.[52] Even the basic problem needs intellectual attention. Should we not insist that wealth needs to be created in a *sustainable* way, and distributed *equably* or *justly*? Is it not important to require that the basic problem of economics be set within, and related to, the more general and fundamental problem of living: How can we sustain, create, and enjoy in the best way what is of value in life?

What is so shocking is that, from its Enlightenment roots in the 18th century onwards, economics has been, and continues to be, conducted as a *science* within the framework of knowledge-inquiry, the basic aim being to improve *knowledge* of economic phenomena.[53] In 2004 I examined 35 introductory textbooks published during the years 1984 to 2003, paying particular attention to how economics is defined. One book on developmental economics suggested that a basic task is to find "appropriate *strategies* for particular countries"[54] — a somewhat wisdom-inquiry formulation. All the other 34 books defined economics in knowledge-inquiry terms as having, as its basic task, to improve knowledge of economic phenomena.[55] Recently I examined 20 introductory books published between 2004 and 2012. Seventeen assumed economics seeks to improve knowledge, while three were more ambivalent. None advocated wisdom economics. As a result of being pursued as a *science*, or a branch of knowledge, economics fails to engage with, or marginalizes, the vital intellectual tasks (1) and (2). This long-standing, gross irrationality of the discipline of economics undoubtedly has much to do with our failure to develop a more sustainable, just, and cooperative global economy than the one we have at present. In betraying reason, economics betrays humanity. Economics here epitomizes the betrayal of social science in general, and academia as a whole.

The Wisdom-Inquiry University:
Aim-Oriented Rationality

How do social inquiry, the humanities, and other relevant disciplines need to be transformed and conducted so as best to help the world put aim-oriented rationality into practice?

Academia can hardly be in a position to help humanity put aim-oriented rationality (AOR) into practice if it does not do this itself. The first requirement is for academia itself to implement AOR. This means that physics explicitly adopts and implements aim-oriented empiricism—physics becoming natural philosophy as a result. It means that all other branches of natural science put aim-oriented empiricism into practice, thereby explicitly acknowledging problematic metaphysical, scientific, value, and political assumptions inherent in basic aims and priorities of research. Scientific discussion needs to be conducted, broadly speaking, in not just two but *three* domains: evidence, theory, and *aims*—the latter being thrown open to non-scientists to discuss value and political assumptions and objectives inherent in scientific aims. More generally, it means that other branches of academia and academia as a whole are transformed so that the aim of acquiring knowledge becomes the highly problematic aim of seeking and promoting what is of value in life, wisdom, progress towards as good a world as possible. AOR needs to be put into practice throughout academia.[56]

This, let us suppose, has been done.[57] Universities are, what at present they are not, shining exemplars of rationality, ideals of rationality to which the rest of the world should seek to aspire. How can academics help our social world put AOR into practice, in the interests of people achieving what is of value in life?

In some areas of social life, AOR may be welcomed, even if it proves difficult to practice, whereas in other areas it will be resisted. We all as individuals want to achieve what is genuinely of value in life. We all at best grow old and die, and everything we achieve, for most of us, if not for all of us, eventually comes to nothing. Our life aims must inevitably be problematic. We might all benefit from putting some elements of AOR into practice in our lives, and yet most of us probably would not take kindly to the suggestion that we misconceive what is in our best interests, and do not quite know how we should be living. We need to create, perhaps, a culture that encourages AOR approaches to life so that learning how to live is generally understood to be a normal part of life, and not something restricted to therapy and the psychoanalytic couch. AOR would also seem to be especially relevant to personal relationships, to the institution of marriage, and to family life. It is clearly relevant to education, for pupil, for teacher, and for educational theory.[58]

In other areas of life, especially the commercial and political, much more resistance, or denial, will be encountered. This is likely to arise whenever the interests of those who govern some endeavour do not accord with the interests of those the endeavour is supposed to serve. Officially, a business serves the interests of its customers, but actually the aim is profit for owners, shareholders, or managing directors. A business will not take kindly to the suggestion that the interests of customers will be better served if modified aims are pursued when this involves less profit. Officially, governments serve the interests of the electorate, but actually a major aim of governments is to stay in power, even if this is at the expense of the real interests of a majority of the electorate. Governments may profess to serve the nation, but will not take kindly to suggestions as to how this service can be improved if the outcome is loss of power, or decrease in likelihood of being re-elected. Oil companies and coal mining companies tend to deny that their activities help to promote global warming. Whenever those governing some endeavour have interests somewhat at odds with the interests of those the endeavour is supposed to serve, there will be a reluctance to put AOR into practice, or even acknowledge that any such thing is desirable. This applies to some extent to science, and to academic inquiry. Scientists may claim that science is for humanity, but the interests of scientists themselves are not always perfectly aligned with the interests of humanity. A science devoted to humanity would put the interests of those whose needs are greatest, the poor of the earth, high on its list of priorities. But modern science is expensive. It is conducted in the main in wealthy nations and tends, as a result, to reflect the interests of the wealthy, the powerful, and scientists themselves, rather than the poor.[59] As in other spheres of life, in science too the interests of those who govern and do the endeavour are not the same as the interests of those the endeavour is supposed to serve.

The first task of AOR social inquiry or philosophy, in these circumstances, is to attempt to discover what the aims of the endeavour in question ought to be, granted that the fundamental aim is to make the appropriate contribution to as good a world as possible. What ought, ideally, to be the aim of business, finance, agriculture, law, government, industry, the media, the military, the arts, science, medicine, technological innovation, granted that the fundamental aim is to contribute to the enrichment of human life in the best possible way? What ought the aim of this specific firm, bank, farm, etc. to be? Ideal aims need to be specified in a hierarchical, AOR fashion, and are, of course, open to revision and improvement.

Discrepancies between what the institution or endeavour itself officially holds its aim to be, and what our best idea is as to the ideal aim, are of interest; but of greater importance are discrepancies between the ideal aim and *actions* of the institution. Deeds are what matter. The deeds in question may be such as to provoke habitat destruction, pollution, global warming, financial instability, unacceptable inequality, harsh treatment of employees, misleading advertising, and so on. Given the contexts we are considering, it is unreasonable to suppose the institution will, of itself, on a voluntary basis, implement required reform when discrepancies between ideal aims, and aims actually being pursued based on actions, are pointed out. Regulatory bodies are required, empowered by legislation, to penalize those enterprises which perform unacceptable actions or fail to implement reforms. This at least is what is required for the private sector. Taxation can be employed as well to discourage undesirable commercial activity. Such measures will be opposed, by business and those on the right wing of politics, who invariably complain of the economically stultifying impact of "red tape" and regulation. But there is no such thing as an unregulated market or capitalist system: it is always a question of how much regulation, of what kind, and applied to what. And if regulation has its negative effects, it must be remembered that this is true of all legislation, the real issue being to find the right balance between negative and positive outcomes. If free enterprise leads to climate change, habitat destruction and extinction of species, increased inequality within and between nations, and all the further undesirable consequences associated with these outcomes, then the operations of the market do indeed need to be regulated, and the gains in human welfare clearly outweigh whatever negative consequences regulation may have.

As academia comes to give far greater prominence than at present to the AOR work I have just indicated — work that would include advocacy of regulation where required — right wing politicians, media, and commentators can be expected to react with outrage at the way — so it will be shouted — the objectivity of universities has been subverted by rampant socialism. In order to counter this charge, it is essential to depict the divergent futures we are likely to encounter, depending on the extent to which we do, or do not, regulate private enterprise. Quite generally, vivid depiction of future possibilities, future scenarios, which become less or more likely depending on what we do now and in the future, becomes a vital task for a kind of social inquiry that is devoted to helping humanity gain wise control of its future—wisdom social inquiry, in other words.

Things become more difficult when the task is to regulate the activities of very wealthy multinational corporations, able to move their activities from one country to another. Here, international agreement of governments from many countries may be necessary, though regulatory action of individual governments may not lead to the departure of the target multinational that is always threatened whenever such regulatory action is mooted.

It needs to be much more widely appreciated, I think, that commercial enterprises vary enormously in the extent to which they do, or do not, make a contribution towards a good world. Some are only interested in profit, and are indifferent to the environmental and social distress that they cause. Others are actively concerned about environmental and welfare matters and seek, in their products and activities, to help us move towards a better future. Muhammad Yunus, creator of the Grameen Bank in Bangladesh, makes out a convincing case for "social businesses"—businesses run for the good of humanity and not to make a profit.[60] One way in which academics could help create an economic system that works in all our best interests (and not primarily in the interests of the wealthy few) would be to develop an accessible, popular critical literature that praises firms that do good work, and criticizes firms that do not and are interested primarily in profit. Science owes its immense intellectual success in part to its institutionalization of criticism. Politics has its critics; and so does literature, theatre, music, and film, but economic activity much more generally does not seem to be subjected to public criticism in the same way—unless in the restricted terms of economic success and failure on the financial pages of newspapers. And yet the whole idea of the free market is that it produces what is of real value because people make informed choices about what to purchase. But if that mechanism is to work properly, a good, accessible, popular critical literature is needed, able to assess well the value of products and of firms.[61]

Getting the public sector to put AOR into practice poses somewhat different problems to the private sector, in that economic penalties are hardly applicable (except, perhaps, where there are internal markets, as in the case of the National Health System of the UK). Regulatory bodies can still operate — and do operate.

Regulation of governments is a different matter. Governments govern themselves. It is, however, a basic task of wisdom-inquiry academia as a whole to get across to government, parliament, the civil service, political parties, and the public what policies need to be adopted and implemented, what legislation needs to be enacted, to enable the nation in particular, and humanity more generally, to make progress towards as good a world as possible. It is to be hoped that this task would be helped by the shadow national government within academia, item 22 in the list of changes required to create wisdom-inquiry of chapter two. Enlightened electorates are all important. Democratic governments do respond to popular demand.

Undemocratic governments are another matter. Dictatorships would not permit wisdom-inquiry to be established in the nation's universities, and would stifle proposals and criticism that wisdom-inquiry would produce. Democratic nations need to do much more than they do at present to help people taken hostage by dictatorships to overthrow them and establish democracy. The Afghanistan and Iraq wars of 2001 and 2003 are glaring examples of what should not be done. Recent events in Tunisia, Libya, Egypt, and Syria — I am writing in 2013 — highlight just how difficult it is to abolish an undemocratic government and establish democracy.

Conclusion

We are confronted by grave global problems. If we are to tackle them effectively and wisely, thus making progress towards as good a world as possible, we need to learn how to do it. That in turn requires that our institutions of learning, our schools and universities, are rationally organized for, and devoted to, the task. At present they are not. Priority needs to be given to tackling problems of living, above all our grave global problems. The basic intellectual aim needs to be to help people realize what is of value in their lives, the scientific pursuit of knowledge and understanding being undertaken as an aspect of that endeavour. A basic task needs to be to help people around the world acquire a good understanding of what our global problems are and what we need to do about them. It needs to be recognized much more widely that the kind of academic inquiry we have inherited from the past — knowledge-inquiry — is damagingly irrational, in a wholesale, structural way, when judged from this standpoint. The long-standing, successful pursuit of scientific knowledge and technological know-how dissociated from a more fundamental concern with problems of living is a key factor in the creation of our current global problems, and our current incapacity to resolve them. As an urgent matter, we need to put wisdom-inquiry into practice in schools and universities around the world. We need a change of paradigm, an academic revolution. This would affect, to a greater or lesser extent, every branch and aspect of academia. Above all, it would put tackling problems of living — global problems — at the heart of the academic enterprise. It would transform the relationship between universities and the social world — universities becoming fundamentally concerned to promote public understanding of what needs to be done to create a better, wiser world. We urgently need a high profile campaign to bring wisdom-inquiry to our universities. This revolution needs to be brought about by helping the kind of research and public education we require to flourish and grow.

Notes

1   Wisdom social inquiry does already exist. There are countless recent publications that seek, in diverse ways, to help humanity resolve its conflicts and problems of living in increasingly cooperatively rational ways. It is just that the academic framework needed to support properly this work does not exist, or at least is seriously deformed by the long-standing dominance of knowledge-inquiry in our universities. There is, I believe, a fund of wisdom-inquiry creative energy, activity, and passion in academia struggling to find expression, at present frustrated and gagged by the prevalence of knowledge-inquiry edicts. When the academic revolution happens, knowledge-inquiry is tossed aside and wisdom-inquiry comes to be generally accepted and implemented, there will be, I believe, a tremendous release of pent-up intellectual energy and creativity, a new renaissance.

2   For an excellent history of the discovery of global warming see Weart (2003).

3   The following sketch of the consequences of rising temperatures from one to six degrees owes much to Mark Lynas's brilliant and terrifying account in his *Six Degrees*, Lynas (2008), in turn based on the work of many climate scientists. I have also consulted the fourth report of the Intergovernmental Panel on Climate Change (IPCC), published in 2007, and the draft of the US National Climate Assessment, published in January 2013.

4   "Ocean surface waters have become 30% more acidic as they have absorbed large amounts of carbon dioxide from the atmosphere", US National Climate Assessment Draft Report (2013), p. 4.

5   Rising temperatures heat up the oceans, which causes the water to expand, and this contributes to rising sea levels.

6   Sea levels have already risen by 8 inches since reliable records began in 1880. The US National Climate Assessment Draft Report (2013, pp. 20–1) estimates that sea levels will rise by somewhere between 1 and 4 feet by the end of the century, and may even rise by as much as 6 feet. Melting of ice in Greenland and Antarctica has already been much more rapid than expected by climate scientists; if this continues, sea levels may rise even more rapidly than that predicted.

7   Thomas (2004).

8   Cox (2000).

9   See http://www.globalpost.com/dispatch/news/science/130118/amazon-rainforest-degrading-climate-change-nasa-says.

10   Lynas (2008, p. 151).

11   For a gripping account of the Permian mass extinction, see Benton (2003).

12   The Guardian, 18 January 2013: http://www.guardian.co.uk/environment/2013/jan/18/amazon-rainforest-climate-change-nasa.

13   Cronin (2010, p. 23 and ch. 9).
14   For an excellent summary of what is known about past changes in
      climate and their relevance to the problem we face today, plus many
      references, see Geology Society of London (2010). The statement con-
      cludes, "Over at least the last 200 million years the fossil and sedi-
      mentary record shows that the Earth has undergone many fluctu-
      ations in climate, from warmer than the present climate to much
      colder, on many different timescales. Several warming events can be
      associated with increases in the 'greenhouse gas' CO_2. There is evid-
      ence for sudden major injections of carbon to the atmosphere occur-
      ring at 55, 120 and 183 million years ago, perhaps from the sudden
      breakdown of methane hydrates beneath the seabed. At those times
      the associated warming would have increased the evaporation of
      water vapour from the ocean, making CO_2 the trigger rather than the
      sole agent for change". For evidence that increased CO_2 caused
      temperature increase 40 million years ago, see Bijl *et al.* (2010).
15   James Hanson, Mark Lynas, and others argue that CO_2 needs to be
      kept to 350 ppm: see www.350.org/ and Lynas (2011, ch. 3). At the
      time of writing we are 45 ppm above this safe upper limit: see
      http://co2now.org/.
16   Stern (2007).
17   See, for example, http://www.transitionnetwork.org/.
18   From 1993 to 2002: average yearly increase 1.67 ppm. Total increase:
      16.73 ppm.
19   Between 2002 and 2010, wealthy individuals in the US channelled
      nearly $120 million to think tanks to spread climate change denial
      propaganda: see Goldenberg (2013).
20   See Hatfield-Dodds (2003) and Rogelj (2013).
21   Better perhaps to tax *consumption* of carbon rather than *emission*.
      From 1990 to 2005 in the UK, emissions went down by 15% but con-
      sumption went up by around 19%, because of goods made in China
      and elsewhere but consumed in the UK: see Helm (2012).
22   See Hillman (2004).
23   See Chichilnisky and Sheeran (2009, p. 9).
24   By "civilized" world I mean simply "good" world, and not merely a
      world that is industrially advanced and has elaborate social and pol-
      itical structures — but may also be more or less barbaric in the way it
      launches aggressive wars or combats terrorism, as the UK and the
      USA may be held to be, in recent years: see, for example, Maxwell
      (2007c).
25   See, however, Lyan (2012).
26   The point is quite general: when it comes to all problematic, worth-
      while aims and ideals — democracy, peace, justice — we need to emp-

loy aim-oriented rationality in seeking to characterize, and realize, them.

27 This is the key idea of aim-oriented empiricism and aim-oriented rationalism: both constitute meta-methodologies designed to facilitate the improvement of (more or less specific) aims and methods in the light of the success they promote, or fail to promote, so that we improve methods for achieving progress as we make progress. Unfortunately we are, at the time of writing, so far from appreciating the significance of this positive feedback conception of rationality, designed to facilitate the improvement of progress-achieving methods in the light of progress we achieve, that it has not even been understood by scientists to be the key idea of scientific rationality, responsible for the explosive growth in scientific knowledge — despite my four decade attempt to get the idea across. (I first argued for aim-oriented empiricism in Maxwell (1972 and 1974).)

28 There is growing inequality in China too, especially between wealthy city dwellers and peasants working the land.

29 Robert Reich, quoted in 'The movie exposing the lie at the heart of US capitalism', *The Observer*, 3 February 2013.

30 See Meacher (2012).

31 See Wilkinson and Pickett (2010).

32 For a brief account of Mondragon see Maxwell (2007, pp. 189–90). For more detailed accounts see MacLeod (1997) and Cheney (2002). For a critical look see Kasmir (1996). For a recent, brief, but enthusiastic look at Mondragon see Wolff (2012).

33 Elsewhere I have argued in more detail that cooperative rationality is required to maximize individual liberty: see Maxwell (1984, pp. 198–9, or 2007a, pp. 221–2).

34 A basic theme of my *From Knowledge to Wisdom* is that we need businesses, institutions, social arrangements, and a culture that encourage and facilitate cooperative rationality, qualified as necessary, wisdom-inquiry and aim-oriented rationality playing a vital role in helping us learn how to bring it about: see Maxwell (1984 or 2007a).

35 See Maxwell (1984 or 2007a, ch. 10; 2001, ch. 2; 2010a, ch. 4). See also Maxwell (1999).

36 I have developed the argument that colours and other perceptual qualities exist in the world around us in the following publications: Maxwell (1966; 1968b; 2000b; 2001, pp. 97–100 & 112–21; 2011c; and especially 2010a, ch. 3). See also Maxwell (2009b; and 2012a).

37 Maxwell (1984, p. 248; or 2007a, p. 269).

38 Pirsig (1974).

39 For more along these lines see Maxwell (2001, pp. 22–4; 2010a, pp.

90–103).

40 I discuss this problem, and argue that it is our fundamental problem, in Maxwell (2010a; 2001). See also Maxwell (1966; 1968a; 1968b; 1980; 1984 or 2007a, ch. 10; 2000b; 2009b; 2011c; 2012a).

41 For a brief account of the disintegration of natural philosophy into science and philosophy, and the need to recreate natural philosophy, see Maxwell (2012c). For a much more detailed exposition of the argument that problem (2a) — the "human world/physical universe" problem — is indeed the fundamental problem of philosophy, properly conceived, and my attempts to solve the problem, see previous note.

42 See Maxwell (2001), especially chs. 1–5; and Maxwell (2010a), especially chs. 3 and 7. See also Maxwell (1966; 1968a; 1968b; 2000b; and 2011c).

43 In reinterpreting Darwinian theory in this way, it is essential to observe the following Principle of Non-Circularity: the theory must not presuppose what it seeks to explain. If purposive action is used to explain some evolutionary development, the theory must explain how this kind of purposive action has itself evolved *without it being presupposed by this explanation*: see Maxwell (2010a, pp. 266–7).

44 There are two ways of thinking of "cultural evolution" — as it is usually called. On the one hand, one may hold that cultural evolution involves the evolution of a new kind of entity, not a living thing, but an item of culture or a characteristic item of behaviour, a "meme" as Richard Dawkins has dubbed it. In my view, however, this is the wrong way to construe what is involved, or the wrong thing to emphasize at least. The right way is to see "evolution by cultural means" (as I prefer to call it to mark the distinction) is as a new mechanism of inheritance, a new mechanism of transmitting a way of life from one generation to the next, grafted on top of genetic inheritance. One generation learns new actions, which the next generation then acquires by means of imitation.

45 See, for example, Dawkins (1978; 1982, pp. 109–12). For a detailed discussion of this neglect of the role of purposivness in evolution, and the vital role of evolution by cultural means, see Maxwell (2010a, ch. 8). I there distinguish nine versions of Darwinian theory, the first giving no role for purposiveness at all, each subsequent version giving an increasingly important role to purposiveness.

46 See Maxwell (2010a, pp. 276–80).

47 See Maxwell (2010a, pp. 274–5).

48 See Maxwell (1984, pp. 181–9 and 259–75, or 2007a, pp. 205–13 and 280–96; 2001, ch. 5).

49 See for example Churchland (1994, p. 308).

50   This is but a bare summary of what is argued for in much greater detail in works referred to in the previous but one note.
51   Experts are needed in sustainable power production — wind, tides, waves, hydroelectric, solar, nuclear, fusion, geothermal, biomass; experts are needed in energy efficiency and communications.
52   This appeals simply to the first two rules of rational problem-solving formulated in chapter two.
53   See Maxwell (1984, pp. 137–9), brought more up to date in Maxwell (2007a, pp. 157–9 and 165–71). For evidence that knowledge-inquiry prevails in academia more generally, see Maxwell (1984, ch. 6, or better 2007a, ch. 6).
54   Norton and Alwang (1993, p. 105). See also Maxwell (2007a, p. 170).
55   See Maxwell (2007a, pp. 165–71).
56   Aim-oriented empiricism is a special case of aim-oriented rationality.
57   We are so far away at the time of writing from this state of affairs, even after my forty-year long campaign, that current conceptions of reason — Bayesian, Popperian, rational choice theory, utility theory — do not include even a nod in the direction of AOR. And yet the argument in support of AOR is elementary and decisive. Any conception of rationality which systematically leads one astray cannot be valid. Whenever we pursue an aim we have mistakenly judged to be in our best interests (as will often happen, aims often being problematic), and the conception of rationality we employ does not include strategies for improving our aim, the more we act in accordance with this conception of rationality in pursuit of our aim, the worse off we will be. Reason becomes not a help but a hindrance. We will be systematically led astray. In order to guard against this it is essential to put AOR into practice whenever aims are problematic (as they often are) — AOR being a conception of rationality that gives us our best help with improving problematic aims. In chapter one I argued that our current global problems are the outcome of our failure to put AOR into practice in economic, industrial, agricultural, political, and financial life.
58   See Maxwell (2005b) for a suggestion concerning education.
59   A point I stressed in chapter two: see note 5 and associated text.
60   See Yunus (2009; 2011).
61   *Which?* is, of course, one attempt to fulfil this need.

References

Most of my papers, and one book, Maxwell (2010a), are available online either at http://philpapers.org/profile/17092 or at http://discovery.ucl.ac.uk/view/people/ANMAX22.date.html

Appleyard, B., 1992, *Understanding the Present: Science and the Soul of Modern Man*, Picador, London.

Aron, R., 1968, *Main Currents in Sociological Thought*, Penguin, Harmondsworth, vol. 1, 1968; vol. 2, 1970.

Barnes, B. and Bloor, D., 1981, 'Relativism, Rationalism and the Sociology of Knowledge' in M. Hollis and S. Lukes, eds., *Rationality and Relativism*, Blackwell, Oxford, pp. 21–47.

Barnes, B., Bloor, D. and Henry, J., 1996, *Scientific Knowledge: A Sociological Analysis,* University of Chicago Press, Chicago.

Barnett, R. and Maxwell, N., eds., 2008, *Wisdom in the University*, Routledge, London.

Barrett, W., 1962, *Irrational Man*, Doubleday, New York.

Benton, M., 2003, *When Life Nearly Died*, Thames and Hudson, London.

Berlin, I., 1979, *Against the Current*, Hogarth Press, London.

Berman, B., 1981, *The Reenchantment of the World*, Cornell University Press, Ithaca.

Bijl, P.K., *et al.*, 2010, 'Transient Middle Eocene Atmospheric CO_2 and Temperature Variations', *Science*, vol. 330, pp. 819–821.

Bloor, D., 1991, *Knowledge and Social Imagery,* 2nd edn., University of Chicago Press, Chicago.

Cheney, G., 2002, *Values at Work*, Cornell University Press, Ithaca.

Chichilnisky, G. and Sheeran, K., 2009, *Saving Kyoto*, New Holland Publishers, London.

Churchland, P., 1994, 'Folk Psychology (2)' in S. Guttenplan, ed., *A Companion to the Philosophy of Mind*, Blackwell, Oxford, pp. 308–316.

Cox, P., 2000, 'Acceleration of Global Warming Due to Carbon Cycle Feedbacks in a Coupled Climate Model', *Nature*, vol. 408, pp. 184–187.

Cronin, T., 2010, *Paleoclimates: Understanding Climate Change Past and Present*, Columbia University Press, New York.

d'Alembert, J., 1963, *Preliminary Discourse to the Encyclopedia of Diderot*, Bobbs-Merrill, New York; originally published in 1751.

Dawkins, R., 1978, *The Selfish Gene*, Paladin, London.

———, 1982, *The Extended Phenotype*, Oxford University Press, Oxford.

Einstein, A., 1949, 'Autobiographical Notes' in P.A. Schilpp, ed., *Albert Einstein: Philosopher-Scientist*, Open Court, Illinois, pp. 3–94.

———, 1973, *Ideas and Opinions*, Souvenir Press, London.

Farganis, J., ed., 1993, *Readings in Social Theory: The Classic Tradition to Post-Modernism*, McGraw-Hill, New York.

Feyerabend, P., 1978, *Against Method*, Verso, London.

———, 1987, *Farewell to Reason*, Verso, London.

Fox Keller, E., 1984, *Reflections on Gender and Science*, Yale University Press, New Haven.

Frisch, M., 1974, *Homo Faber*, Penguin, Harmondsworth.

Gascardi, A., 1999, *Consequences of Enlightenment*, Cambridge University Press, Cambridge.

Gay, P., 1973, *The Enlightenment: An Interpretation*, Wildwood House, London.

Geological Society of London, 2010, 'Climate Change: Evidence from the Geological Record', http://www.geolsoc.org.uk/climatechange.

Goldenberg, S., 2013, 'US "Dark Money" Funds Climate Sceptics', *The Guardian*, 15 February 2013, www.guardian.co.uk/environment/2013/feb/14/funding-climate-change-denial-thinktanks-network.

Gray, J., 2004, *Heresies: Against Progress and Other Illusions*, Granta Books, London.

Gross, P. and Levitt, N., 1994, *Higher Superstition: The Academic Left and Its Quarrels with Science*, John Hopkins University Press, Baltimore.

Gross, P., Levitt, N. and Lewis, M., eds., 1996, *The Flight from Science and Reason*, John Hopkins University Press, Baltimore.

Harding, S., 1986, *The Feminist Question in Science*, Open University Press, Milton Keynes.

Hatfield-Dodds, S., 2013, 'All in the Timing', *Nature,* vol. 493, pp. 35–36.

Hayek, F.A., 1979, *The Counter-Revolution of Science*, 1979, Liberty Press, Indianapolis.

Helm, D., 2012, 'The Kyoto Approach has Failed', *Nature*, vol. 491, pp. 663–665.

Higgins, R., 1978, *The Seventh Enemy: The Human Factor in the Global Crisis*, Hodder and Stoughton, London.

Hillman, M., 2004, *How We Can Save the Planet*, Penguin, London.

Howard, N., 2011, 'We Are a Direct Challenge to the Contemporary Structure of Mainstream Universities', *The Guardian*, 16 November, www.guardian.co.uk/commentisfree/2011/nov/15/welfare-education-law-occupy-london.

Iredale, M., 2007, 'From Knowledge-Inquiry to Wisdom-Inquiry: Is the Revolution Underway?', *London Review of Education*, vol. 5, pp. 117–129; reprinted in Barnett and Maxwell, 2008, pp. 21–33.

Kasmir, S., 1996, *The Myth of Mondragon*, State University of New York Press, Albany.

Koertge, N., ed., 1998, *A House Built on Sand*, Oxford University Press, Oxford.

Laing, R.D., 1965, *The Divided Self*, Penguin, Harmondsworth.

Langley, C., 2005, *Soldiers in the Laboratory*, Scientists for Global Responsibility, Folkstone.

Latour, B., 1987, *Science in Action*, Open University Press, Milton Keynes.

Lynas, M., 2008, *Six Degrees*, Harper Perennial, London.

_____, 2012, *The God Species: How Humans Really Can Save the Planet*, Fourth Estate, London.

Macdonald, C., 2009, 'Nicholas Maxwell in Context: The Relationship of His Wisdom Theses to the Contemporary Global Interest in Wisdom', in L. McHenry, 2009, pp. 61–81.

MacLeod, G., 1997, *From Mondragon to America*, University College of Cape Breton Press, Sydney, Nova Scotia.

Marcuse, H., 1964, *One Dimensional Man*, Beacon Press, Boston.

Maxwell, N., 1966, 'Physics and Common Sense', *British Journal for the Philosophy of Science,* vol. 16, pp. 295–311.

_____, 1968a, 'Can there be Necessary Connections Between Successive Events?', *British Journal for the Philosophy of Science*, vol. 19, pp. 1–25.

_____, 1968b, 'Understanding Sensations', *Australasian Journal of Philosophy,* vol. 46, pp. 127–146.

_____, 1972, 'A New Look at the Quantum Mechanical Problem of Measurement', *American Journal of Physics*, vol. 40, pp. 1431–1435.

_____, 1974, 'The Rationality of Scientific Discovery', *Philosophy of Science,* vol. 41, pp. 123–153 and 247–295.

_____, 1976a, *What's Wrong With Science?*, Bran's Head Books, Frome, England; 2nd ed., 2009, Pentire Press, London.

_____, 1976b, 'Towards a Micro Realistic Version of Quantum Mechanics, Parts I and II', *Foundations of Physics,* vol. 6, pp. 275–292 and 661–676.

_____, 1980, 'Science, Reason, Knowledge and Wisdom: A Critique of Specialism', *Inquiry,* vol. 23, pp. 19–81.

_____, 1982, 'Instead of Particles and Fields', *Foundations of Physics,* vol. 12, pp. 607–631.

_____, 1984, *From Knowledge to Wisdom: A Revolution in the Aims and Methods of Science*, Blackwell, Oxford.

_____, 1988, 'Quantum Propensiton Theory: A Testable Resolution of the Wave/Particle Dilemma', *British Journal for the Philosophy of Science*, vol. 39, pp. 1–50.

_____, 1992, 'What Kind of Inquiry Can Best Help Us Create a Good World?', *Science, Technology and Human Values,* vol. 17, pp. 205–227.

_____, 1993, 'Induction and Scientific Realism: Einstein versus van Fraassen', *British Journal for the Philosophy of Science,* vol. 44, pp. 61–79, 81–101, and 275–305.

_____, 1994, 'Particle Creation as the Quantum Condition for Probabilistic Events to Occur', *Physics Letters A,* vol. 187, pp. 351–355.

_____, 1998, *The Comprehensibility of the Universe,* Oxford University Press, Oxford; pbk. 2003.

_____, 1999, 'Are there Objective Values?', *The Dalhousie Review,* vol. 79 (3), pp. 301–317.

_____, 2000a, 'Can Humanity Learn to Become Civilized? The Crisis of Science Without Civilization', *Journal of Applied Philosophy,* vol. 17, pp. 29–44.

_____, 2000b, 'The Mind–Body Problem and Explanatory Dualism', *Philosophy,* vol. 75, pp. 49–71.

_____, 2001, *The Human World in the Physical Universe,* Rowman and Littlefield, Lanham.

_____, 2002, 'The Need for a Revolution in the Philosophy of Science', *Journal for General Philosophy of Science,* vol. 33, pp. 381–408.

_____, 2004a, *Is Science Neurotic?,* Imperial College Press, London.

_____, 2004b, 'Does Probabilism Solve the Great Quantum Mystery?', *Theoria,* vol. 19/3, no. 51, pp. 321–336.

_____, 2005a, 'Popper, Kuhn, Lakatos and Aim-Oriented Empiricism', *Philosophia,* vol. 32, pp. 181–239.

_____, 2005b, 'Philosophy Seminars for Five-Year-Olds', *Learning for Democracy,* vol. 1, no. 2, pp. 71–77; republished in *Gifted Education International,* vol. 22, no. 2/3, 2007, pp. 122–127.

_____, 2007a, *From Knowledge to Wisdom: A Revolution for Science and the Humanities,* Pentire Press, London; 2nd revised and extended edition of Maxwell, 1984.

_____, 2007b, 'From Knowledge to Wisdom: The Need for an Academic Revolution', *London Review of Education,* vol. 5, no. 2, pp. 97–115; reprinted in Barnett and Maxwell, 2008, pp. 1–19.

_____, 2007c, 'The Disastrous War against Terrorism: Violence versus Enlightenment', ch. 3 of *Terrorism Issues: Threat Assess-*

ment, Consequences and Prevention, ed. Albert W. Merkidze, Nova Science Publishers, New York, pp. 111–133.

————, 2008, 'Do We Need a Scientific Revolution?', *Journal for Biological Physics and Chemistry*, vol. 8, no. 3, pp. 95–105.

————, 2009a, 'Are Universities Undergoing an Intellectual Revolution?', *Oxford Magazine*, No. 290, Eighth Week, Trinity Term, June, pp. 13–16.

————, 2009b, 'How Can Life of Value Best Flourish in the Real World?', in McHenry, 2009, pp. 1–56.

————, 2010a, *Cutting God in Half – And Putting the Pieces Together Again: A New Approach to Philosophy*, Pentire Press, London.

————, 2010b, 'Wisdom Mathematics', *Friends of Wisdom Newsletter*, No. 6, pp. 1–6, www.knowledgetowisdom.org/Newsletter%206.pdf.

————, 2011a, 'A Priori Conjectural Knowledge in Physics' in M. Shaffer and M. Veber, eds., *What Place for the A Priori?*, Open Court, Chicago, pp. 211–240.

————, 2011b, 'Is the Quantum World Composed of Propensitons?' in M. Suárez, ed., *Probabilities, Causes and Propensities in Physics*, Synthese Library, Springer, Dordrecht, pp. 221–243.

————, 2011c, 'Three Philosophical Problems about Consciousness and their Possible Resolution', *Open Journal of Philosophy*, vol. 1, no. 1, pp. 1–10.

————, 2012a, 'Arguing for Wisdom in the University: An Intellectual Autobiography', *Philosophia*, vol. 40, no. 4.

————, 2012b, 'How Universities Can Help Humanity Learn How to Resolve the Crises of Our Times – From Knowledge to Wisdom: The University College London Experience' in D. Rooney *et al.*, eds., *Handbook on the Knowledge Economy*, vol. 2, Edward Elgar Publishing Inc., Cheltenham, pp. 158–179.

————, 2012c, 'In Praise of Natural Philosophy: A Revolution for Thought and Life', *Philosophia*, vol. 40, no. 4, pp. 705–715.

————, 2013, 'Has Science Established that the Cosmos is Physically Comprehensible?' in A Travena and B. Soren, eds., *Recent Advances in Cosmology*, Nova Science Publishers, New York, http://discovery.ucl.ac.uk/1369638/.

Meacher, M., 2012, 'Britain's 1,000 Richest Persons Made Gains of £155bn in Last 3 Years', http://www.michaelmeacher.info/weblog/2012/04/britains-1000-richest-persons-made-gains-of-155bn-in-last-3-years/.

McHenry, L., ed., 2009, *Science and the Pursuit of Wisdom: Studies in the Philosophy of Nicholas Maxwell*, Ontos Verlag, Frankfurt.

Norton, G. and Alwang, J., 1993, *Introduction to Economics of Agricultural Development*, McGraw-Hill, New York.

Nowotny, H., Scott, P. and Gibbons, M., 2001, *Re-Thinking Science*, Polity Press, Cambridge.

Penrose, R., 2004, *The Road to Reality*, Jonathan Cape, London.

Pickering, A., 1984, *Constructing Quarks*, University of Chicago Press, Chicago.

Pinker, S., 2011, *The Better Angels of Our Nature*, Allen Lane, London.

Pirsig, R., 1974, *Zen and the Art of Motorcycle Maintenance*, Bodley Head, London.

Popper, K.R., 1959, *The Logic of Scientific Discovery*, Hutchinson, London.

———, 1961, *The Poverty of Historicism*, Routledge and Kegan Paul, London.

———, 1962, *The Open Society and Its Enemies*, Routledge and Kegan Paul, London.

———, 1963, *Conjectures and Refutations*, Routledge and Kegan Paul, London.

Rogers, P.F., 2006, 'Peace Studies' in A. Collins, ed., *Contemporary Security Studies,* Oxford University Press, Oxford, ch. 3.

Roszak, T., 1973, *Where the Wasteland Ends*, Faber and Faber, London.

Rgelj, J., *et al.*, 2013, 'Probabilistic Cost Estimates for Climate Change Mitigation', *Nature,* 493, pp. 79–83.

Ryle, G., 1949, *The Concept of Mind*, Hutchinson, London.

Schwartz, B., 1987, *The Battle for Human Nature*, W.W. Norton, New York.

Segerstrale, U., 2000, *Science Wars*, State University of New York Press, Albany.

Shapin, S., 1994, *A Social History of Truth*, University of Chicago Press, Chicago.

Shapin, S. and Schaffer, S., 1985, *Leviathan and the Airpump*, Princeton University Press, Princeton.

Smith, D., 2003, *The Atlas of War and Peace*, Earthscan, London.

Snow, C.P., 1986, *The Two Cultures: And a Second Look*, Cambridge University Press, Cambridge.

Sokal, A. and Bricmont, J., 1998, *Intellectual Impostures*, Profile Books, London.

Stern, N., 2007, *The Economics of Climate Change: The Stern Review*, Cambridge University Press, Cambridge, www.hm-treasury. gov.uk/sternreview_index.htm.

Sternberg, R.J., ed., 1990, *Wisdom: Its Nature, Origins and Development,* Cambridge University Press, Cambridge.

Sternberg, R.J., *et al.*, 2007, 'Teaching for Wisdom: What Matters Is Not Just What Students Know, But How They Use It', *London Review of Education*, vol. 5, pp. 143–158.

Thomas, C., *et al.*, 2004, 'Extinction Risk from Climate Change', *Nature*, vol. 427, pp. 145–148.

US National Climate Assessment Draft Report, 2013, http://ncadac. globalchange.gov/

Weart, S., 2003, *The Discovery of Global Warming*, Harvard University Press, Cambridge, MA.

Wilkinson, R. and Pickett, K., 2010, *The Spirit Level*, Penguin, London.

Wilsdon, J. and Willis, R., 2004, *See-through Science*, Demos, London.

Wolff, R., 2012, 'Yes, There is an Alternative to Capitalism: Mondragon Shows the Way', http://www.guardian.co.uk/ commentisfree/2012/jun/24/alternative-capitalism-mondragon

Yunus, M., 2009, *Creating a World Without Poverty: Social Business and the Future of Capitalism*, Public Affairs, New York, http:// tamannah.files.wordpress.com/2011/11/personalities-muhammad-yunus-creating-a-world-without-poverty.pdf.

_____, 2011, *Building Social Business: The New Kind of Capitalism that Serves Humanity's Most Pressing Needs*, Public Affairs, New York.

Zamyatin, Y., 1972, *We*, Penguin, Harmondsworth.

Index

24, 38, 42, 77–8, 94, 113
and feelings and desires
38–9, 40–2, 58
and global problems 5, 11,
21, 24–5, 66–84
and government 60, 78, 95
and mathematics 59
and natural science 29, 31–
4, 43–4, 47–9, 52–4, 55, 57
and philosophy 37–8, 59,
120–2
and politics 58, 60, 61, 68,
79–80, 114–16
and problems of living 27–
9, 44–7, 75–81, 94–5, 114,
120, 124–6, 128–31
and public education 16–
17, 37–8, 58, 67–8, 77–8, 84,
94–5, 115, 138
and role of pure science
43–4, 47–9, 52–4, 55
and social inquiry 37–8, 42,
49–53, 55, 56–7, 94–5, 97–8,
128–37
and social world 27–9, 35–
8, 58, 67–9, 75–81, 94–5, 97–
8

and synthesis of social and
technological 107, 128–31
arguments for 9–12, 20–
47,66–84
cultural implications of
39–44
implementation of 55–60,
118–37
improved version of
knowledge-inquiry 12, 22,
27–9, 55–61
see also academic
revolution, aim-oriented
empiricism, aim-oriented
rationality
Wisdom-Inquiry University
118–37
and aim-pursuing
rationality 132–7
and problem-solving
rationality 118–32
Wisdom Page, The 93
wise world 107–14
Wordsworth, W. 13

Yunus, M. 136

Zamyatin, Y. 13

What critics have said about two of the author's previous books:

From Knowledge to Wisdom
Maxwell is advocating nothing less than a revolution (based on reason, not
on religious or Marxist doctrine) in our intellectual goals and methods of
inquiry… There are altogether too many symptoms of malaise in our
science-based society for Nicholas Maxwell's diagnosis to be ignored.
Professor Christopher Longuet-Higgins, *Nature.*

The essential idea is really so simple, so transparently right… It is a profound
book, refreshingly unpretentious, and deserves to be read, refined and
implemented.
Dr. Stewart Richards, *Annals of Science.*

…a strong effort is needed if one is to stand back and clearly state the
objections to the whole enormous tangle of misconceptions which surround
the notion of science today. Maxwell has made that effort in this powerful,
profound and important book.
Dr. Mary Midgley, *University Quarterly.*

This book is a provocative and sustained argument for a 'revolution', a call
for a 'sweeping, holistic change in the overall aims and methods of institu-
tionalized inquiry and education, from knowledge to wisdom'… Maxwell
offers solid and convincing arguments for the exciting and important thesis
that rational research and debate among professionals concerning values and
their realization is both possible and ought to be undertaken.
Professor Jeff Foss, *Canadian Philosophical Review.*

Wisdom, as Maxwell's own experience shows, has been outlawed from the
western academic and intellectual system… In such a climate, Maxwell's
effort to get a hearing on behalf of wisdom is indeed praiseworthy.
Dr. Ziauddin Sardar, *Inquiry.*

Maxwell has, I believe, written a very important book which will resonate in
the years to come. For those who are not inextricably and cynically locked
into the power and career structure of academia with its government-indus-
trial-military connections, this is a book to read, think about, and act on.
Dr. Brian Easlea, *Journal of Applied Philosophy.*

Maxwell's argument… is a powerful one. His critique of… the philosophy of
knowledge is coherent and well argued, as is his defence of the philosophy

of wisdom… This is an exciting and important work.

Dr. John Hendry, *British Journal for the History of Science.*

This book is written in simple straightforward language… The style is passionate, committed, serious; it communicates Maxwell's conviction that we are in deep trouble, that there is a remedy available, and that it is ingrained bad intellectual habits that prevent us from improving our lot… Maxwell is raising an important and fundamental question and things are not going so well for us that we should afford the luxury of listening only to well-tempered answers.

Professor John Kekes, *Inquiry.*

Any philosopher or other person who seeks wisdom should read this book. Any educator who loves education—especially those in leadership positions—should read this book. Anyone who wants to understand an important source of modern human malaise should read this book. And anyone trying to figure out why, in a world that produces so many technical wonders, there is such an immense 'wisdom gap' should read this book… Maxwell presents a compelling, wise, humane, and timely argument for a shift in our fundamental 'aim of inquiry' from that of knowledge to that of wisdom.

Jeff Huggins, *Metapsychology.*

Is Science Neurotic?

Maxwell has written a very important book… [He] eloquently discusses the astonishing advances and the terrifying realities of science without global wisdom. While science has brought forth significant advancements for society, it has also unleashed the potential for annihilation. Wisdom is now, as he puts it, not a luxury but a necessity.

Professor Joseph Davidow, *Learning for Democracy.*

Is science neurotic? Yes, says Nicholas Maxwell, and the sooner we acknowledge it and understand the reasons why, the better it will be for academic inquiry generally and, indeed, for the whole of humankind. This is a bold claim… But it is also realistic and deserves to be taken very seriously… I found the book fascinating, stimulating and convincing… I have come to see the profound importance of its central message.

Dr. Mathew Iredale, *The Philosopher's Magazine.*